Praise for *Don't Retire Broke*

"*Don't Retire Broke* is not only an easy read, it's an important one! Whether you're just beginning to plan for retirement, in the middle-stages, or nearing the finish-line, *Don't Retire Broke* offers great tips and strategies to ensure your long-term success. And, as if not more importantly, the book also covers all the classic mistakes one can make while planning, with real-life lessons that are sobering yet helpful and can save you thousands. While one can never plan enough for how to manage the 'rest of their life,' this book—and the opportunity to learn from a master like Rick Rodgers—provides a tremendous foundation on which to build. I highly recommend it!"

—Tom Baldrige, president and CEO,
The Lancaster Chamber of Commerce and Industry

"Don't Retire Broke explains how best to maximize your wealth before and after retirement, gives you real life examples of those who could have made better decisions and then gives a defined set of choices for our circumstances. I find it especially thought provoking for small business owners, who make retirement decisions based on very little knowledge or expertise in these matters, and often find themselves at retirement age still trying to determine how best to utilize the funds they have accumulated for retirement. Tax laws are complicated and Rick has done a great job in making this book easy to read and understand for the layman...this book has something for everyone...no matter their financial status."

—Gerard L. Glenn, past chairman of the board,
SCORE Association, SCORE Foundation

DON'T
RETIRE
BROKE

An Indispensible Guide to Tax-Efficient
Retirement Planning and Financial Freedom

RICK RODGERS

CAREER
PRESS
Wayne, NJ

DON'T RETIRE BROKE
EDITED BY JODI BRANDON
TYPESET BY PERFECTYPE, NASHVILLE, TENNESSEE
Cover design by Rob Johnson/Toprotype
Front cover/spine image by Lightspring/shutterstock
Back cover image by Sergey Nivens/shutterstock

Printed in the U.S.A.

To order this title, please call toll-free 1-800-CAREER-1 (NJ and Canada: 201-848-0310) to order using VISA or MasterCard, or for further information on books from Career Press.

The Career Press, Inc.
12 Parish Drive
Wayne, NJ 07470
www.careerpress.com

Library of Congress Cataloging-in-Publication Data
CIP Data Available Upon Request.

This book is dedicated to my wife,
Jessica Rodgers.

CONTENTS

FOREWORD

In *Don't Retire Broke*, Rick Rodgers builds on the strength of his first edition while preserving all of the style and impact of his earlier release. The goal remains the same: Use the investment tools available to maximize your wealth by investing in ways that minimize your tax liability now and in retirement.

My first meetings with Rick were the result of my business as an educator. Eventually, our conversations circled around to his business in wealth management, a subject in which he is well versed. Rick understands that we all want to maximize our wealth, though most of us don't have enough technical expertise to preserve what wealth we have and maximize investments through sound decision-making. Reading *Don't Retire Broke* confirmed my suspicions that I am no exception to this modern-day phenomenon. Rick is a well-known and well-respected wealth manager with an impeccable record of success and ringing endorsements. We are fortunate that he is willing to explain the complexities and intricacies of tax law and the impact they have on investment strategies for the sole purpose of maximizing our assets and minimizing tax liability.

Tax laws are complicated and ever changing. Each of us wants to ensure that we take advantage of every legal means at our disposal to secure the maximum investment of our assets at retirement; but how many of us are achieving that goal, especially with continually changing tax laws? How do we keep pace with all of the modifications that make new opportunities available to us? Rick does an excellent job in demonstrating the myriad of options one has and the implications subtle decisions can make in our retirement portfolio. No two cases are alike. For example, a very simple decision which everyone has to make, but a decision with significant impact, is when to start taking Social Security benefits. Rick methodically takes the reader through the implications of this decision in a very understandable way, complete with graphics and charts. Rick's examples clearly demonstrate that everyone's situation is unique, and early in Rick's writing it becomes abundantly clear how beneficial this book is to improving the quality of one's financial life.

What makes this book credible and comprehensible is the style in which Rick presents the material, which has the scholarly content to be used in college-level investment courses and is yet readable for the lay person. Concepts are rooted in a full understanding of tax law, supplemented with real case studies and easily understandable "Rick's Tips." After reading the book, I recognized that my own "three-legged stool" was quite shaky, and I have made the same mistake as have many others: attempting to maximize pre-tax investments by building 401(k) type accounts to reduce current tax liabilities and failing to think long-term by not balancing my investments through Roth IRAs. Through the case studies one begins to see how minimal changes in investment decisions can make sizeable differences in your retirement and, thus, your quality of life.

No matter the magnitude of your wealth, there is something in Rick's book for everybody. You probably know people in situations similar to those Rick describes throughout *Don't Retire Broke* who would benefit from the material contained in these chapters. This book reminds us all that retirement planning must start early. We can all benefit from reading this book early in our career and using it as a reference in succeeding years to reexamine our investment plans. Fortunately, it is never too late to adjust our strategies. I know I have.

John M. Anderson, Ph.D.
President, Millersville University
Millersville, Pennsylvania

INTRODUCTION:
THE UN-FUNNIEST STORY
EVER TOLD

CASE STUDY
Frank Richardson, Army veteran and business owner

In September 2002, Frank Richardson died of natural causes in Lancaster, Pennsylvania. Frank was a good man who served four years in the United States Army and fought for his country in the Korean War. He then spent 25 years building a successful wholesale lumber business in Lancaster. Frank worked hard to improve both his own life and the lives of others around him, employing 1,000 people in the town—people like you and me who got up every morning, drank coffee, took their kids to school, and built lives.

Unfortunately, Frank didn't work as hard to ensure all of his assets would be available to future generations. In general, he mistrusted financial advisers and never made time for them, a lesson he learned from watching his father follow an adviser's advice yet still lose the family farm during the Great Depression.

Frank believed in only one financial strategy: make no changes. In keeping with this strategy, he trained the people around him never to offer him financial advice. He got his few investment tips from friends at his club and on TV. Only once did a local financial adviser get an audience with Frank and, after reviewing his retirement assets, he told him he could take out a distribution and invest it in one of the mutual funds the adviser was representing. Frank politely escorted the young man to the door.

Frank avoided the subject of his retirement fund, reasoning they had made things way too complicated and always putting it off until later. He chose instead to help people he knew around town whom he claimed had "real" problems. Yet in focusing on the situations of others and never his own, Frank ultimately did wrong for his family.

At the time of his death, Frank Richardson was worth more than $4.4 million, which included his only liquid asset—his IRA—and about $2 million in property. He left everything to his wife, Eleanor. Eleanor also trusted Frank's judgment and left the investments unchanged. Then the unthinkable happened: Eleanor died unexpectedly in 2007.

I was called in as a retirement account specialist to help settle the estate. I'd been invited by Jim Richardson, the eldest of the three surviving children. After a brief look at their records, I noticed neither Frank nor Eleanor had been taking their required minimum distributions (RMDs; I discuss these throughout the book). What Frank and his wife failed to understand is the IRS has the right to levy a 50% penalty for not taking minimum distributions. The Richardson parents could have distributed more than $425,000 among their children without penalty. Unfortunately, the IRS penalty was $212,500 for the missed distribution date—a date totally invented by a bureaucrat and hidden in the fine print!

I showed Jim the place in the IRS rule book where it states a husband and wife can pass an unlimited amount of assets to each other without federal estate or gift taxes. Although there were no estate taxes due upon Frank's death because he left everything to Eleanor, the same didn't hold true for the estate Eleanor left to her family. Instead, the Richardson children were forced to pay an astronomical $1,035,000 federal tax on the estate (a 45% tax was levied on any amount in excess of $2 million in 2002).

Eleanor was also a resident of Pennsylvania, which has an inheritance tax. This tax is based on to whom the money is left. Because lineal descendants in Pennsylvania are taxed at 4.5%, the state charged Eleanor's estate another $202,500. (I told you this wasn't funny!)

The final unfairness was the distribution out of the retirement account, which was taxed as ordinary income. In 2001, Congress set up the AMT (alternative minimum tax), which kept the estate tax from offsetting the IRS's tax on ordinary income. The IRS subsequently charged the Richardson heirs $696,500 in federal income tax, even though some of the income had already been paid in estate taxes. They were essentially paying taxes on taxes!

Fortunately, Pennsylvania doesn't tax income distributed from retirement accounts, but 23 other states, including California, do. If the Richardsons had lived in California, they would've lost an additional $485,000, or 90% of everything—gone!

In the end, the Richardson siblings had to pay a total in taxes and penalties of $2,145,000—totaling 85.8% of their father's retirement account, which was worth about $2,500,000 at the time of Eleanor's death. Because the other $2 million in assets were tied up in property, and the taxes and penalties had to be paid within nine months, they didn't have enough time to sell the properties to help with the payment. Yet if the Richardsons had had other liquid assets to pay the taxes, they wouldn't have had as much income tax to pay.

Saving everything in tax-deferred accounts like the Richardsons did is one of the biggest problems I see in retirement planning. These were good, hardworking people who had conducted themselves honorably throughout their professional lives. They paid their taxes on time, employed local townspeople in their business, and went to church. Their father's only mistake was in not understanding the IRS's basic distribution rules—rules even a first-year financial planning student would've known. Of course, the Richardson children were mad as could be and wanted to take the IRS to court, but what was done, was done.

Rest assured, what I just described is a true story—and not the exception to the rule. A kind heart and an empty head won't stand up in a court of law. Your protection is knowledge. You can either get it from me or someone like me in your own town, but whatever or whomever the source, you need to know your options.

What could the Richardsons have done differently? For starters, a simple action such as a properly drawn will could have provided for the establishment of a credit shelter trust upon Frank's death. When Frank died in 2002, $1 million of property could have been set aside in a credit shelter trust and not been exposed to tax ($1 million was the maximum amount that could avoid estate tax in 2002). The income would still be paid to Eleanor, but this would have removed $1 million from her estate. This step could have saved $360,000 in federal estate taxes alone.

Next, Eleanor should have taken out the RMDs from the retirement account each year; had she done so, she would've saved the $212,500 in tax penalties. She could have put her savings into a passive investment plan (I'll talk more about this in "Leg Two" [Chapter 2] of the book) and possibly made a comfortable annual return. For example, if the amount she lost to penalties had found its way into an investment program earning merely 5%, it would have provided additional income of $10,625 per year. (Of course, that amount would've been taxed, but we'll also discuss more about investments and taxes in Leg Two.)

Because Eleanor didn't need her distribution income, she could have gifted some or all of her distributions to her children and grandchildren. (Gifts can currently be made for up to $14,000 per year to as many individuals you desire without being subject to gift tax.) Had she gifted away the entire minimum distributions each year, she would have saved an additional $225,000 in estate tax.

Finally, Eleanor should have rolled over Frank's retirement account to her name and named her children as beneficiaries. This move would've allowed each child to take minimum distributions over his or her lifetime, delaying the payment of income tax until the money was actually withdrawn from the account each year.

These are easy steps that could have reduced the total federal, inheritance, and income taxes on Frank's IRA to $800,000, or 32%—a whole lot better than 85.8%! Getting this advice from a financial planner would likely have cost him less than $1,000 for a few hours of the planner's time. Even if it cost him $10,000, his family would still have saved more than a million dollars—dollars that instead went to fund government programs, most of which didn't even benefit the great state of Pennsylvania where Frank and Eleanor made their home.

With this book, my goal is to help you retain as much of your hard-earned retirement assets as possible—and to avoid the heartbreaking outcome experienced by the Richardson family. The Three-Legged Stool approach to financial security makes it both easy to understand how to achieve this retirement security and difficult to "lose balance"—that is, to get off-track once you've established your plan.

The book is divided into three main sections representing each of the three "legs," or components, you'll need to have the most tax-effective financial structure:

> **Leg One: Tax-Deferred Savings Strategies.** This section covers how to make the most of your IRA, 401(k), and other tax-deferred retirement vehicles.
>
> **Leg Two: After-Tax Savings Strategies.** In this section, I discuss how to build your investment plan around the important concept of asset allocation; five important risk-reducing investment strategies; and—last but not least—how to structure your investments in the most tax-efficient way possible.
>
> **Leg Three: Tax-Free Savings Strategies.** This section focuses on the smartest tax-free retirement savings methods—the Roth IRA and Roth 401(k)—and how to convert your existing accounts to these fantastic options.

After learning about these three key factors in retirement savings, we'll wrap up the book with discussions about the all-important Retirement Distribution (R/D) Factor and the role it plays in your eventual retirement savings distributions, a closer look at Social Security, and a special bonus section on estate planning. Be sure to keep an eye out for my quick tips along the way, as well as the list of recommendations I include at the end of each section.

The truth, in matters of taxes, is that once the IRS gets its hands on your money, it's lost to the abyss that is the Federal Treasury. You must act before that event takes place—and this book will help you do it. At the end of the day, it's what you and your family get to keep that counts.

Why Would the IRS Take Your Money?

After reading the terrible story about the Richardsons, you're probably asking yourself: What possible motive could the IRS have for taking my retirement money? The answer is simple and straightforward: Our government is going to need your money—and lots of other Americans'—to keep our country running.

As of March 2016, our country's national debt totaled more than $19 trillion (and the number continues to rise by $1 million every minute!). That amounts to $154,200 of debt for each taxpayer in the United States. Yet this is a mere drop in the proverbial bucket compared to what the government will owe in benefits to Social Security and Medicare recipients far into the future, as well as in pensions to military and civilian government workers.

In other words, the true liability of the United States isn't only the Treasury bills, notes, and bonds we sell to finance our annual deficit and keep the country running, but it's also all of the promises we've made to make benefits payments in the future. Plus, we added another expensive piece of legislation with the passage of the Affordable Care Act in 2010. This law is still being implemented, and the final price tag is only a guess at this point. All told, our government's debt list of projects, departments, agencies, bureaus, and programs is a mile long. And where do you think the Treasury is going to get its funding? From *you!*

The wealthiest 25% of Americans pay 86% of the tax bills.[1] And guess what? It's not enough! In view of this statistic, it's easy to see the IRS's motive for wanting to take as much of your retirement money as possible.

At this point, you may be thinking, *but I'm not wealthy.* Sorry—it doesn't take a lot to be rich in the eyes of the IRS. Simply having your name on an IRA or 401(k) plan distribution list makes you a target. The IRS sees a huge amount of collective dollars—$24.2 trillion[2], to be exact—stashed away in IRAs and retirement programs. This has caused it to become extremely aggressive in taxing those assets. So you may not like it, but believe me, it's true: The IRS has a big red bull's-eye painted on your retirement plan.

Our individual state governments also have a hand out. Why? Because they have been losing money for many of the same reasons the country has—and the largest revenue losses are just beginning as the Baby Boomer generation retires and states begin to face the higher costs and other issues associated with that retirement. Baby Boomers have been turning age 65 at a rate of 8,000 a day since 2011.[3] Costs for state pensions and retiree health insurance will increase as Baby Boomers age. States will bear a particularly heavy burden for health care for the aging population, because it's the states' Medicaid programs (rather than federally run Medicare) that pay for long-term care. The significant revenue losses these budget proposals will engender will make it still more difficult for states to meet these responsibilities.

It may not seem fair, but we have little control over it. What each of us does have control over is taking the right steps toward protecting retirement assets from excessive taxation—taxes you may not even know you owe.

Who Am I to Give You Advice?

My job as both a financial adviser and the author of *Don't Retire Broke* is to provide asset protection solutions that truly work. My many years of success at this have been recognized throughout the industry. Since the first edition of my book came out in 2009, I have become a regular guest on various regional and national television news programs, noted for my expert commentary on retirement planning and tax strategy. Millions of people have heard or seen me on radio and television coast to coast on such networks and shows as FOX Business, MSNBC, and the *700 Club*. My articles have appeared in *Wealth Manager, CPA Magazine,* and *Medical Economics*; and I've been quoted in the *New York Times, Investment News, Smart Money,* and others.

If you need more to go on than an endorsement from some of the nation's foremost media publications, don't worry, because I'm going to tell you how you can test my ideas yourself. You'll be able to do this by following the very specific course of action I lay out in the pages of this book. It won't be a general approach to the game of beating the IRS; developing a solid asset protection plan isn't like a tennis match, for instance, where your strategy might be "play aggressively" or "play safe shots." Rather, the following sections will give you a defined set of choices to make for many circumstances that might arise.

The New Three-Legged Stool™ Approach to Financial Security

Imagine you're playing a game called Retirement Distribution. Your opponent, the IRS, wrote the rules of the game. The rule book is more than 70,000 pages with more than 10 million words.[4] Since 2001, there have been nearly 5,000 changes to the tax code—about one change a day. No individual can hope to keep up with it. American taxpayers spend 6.1 billion hours each year in tax preparation and compliance. That's enough time to keep 3 million full-time employees working for a year. The secret to winning this game is to keep the IRS out of your financial affairs before it has the right to interfere. My role in the game is to explain the fine print in the rule book and to provide you with a strategy that covers many eventualities, so in the end, you win the game.

As I mentioned earlier, this book focuses on three strategies that can help you emerge victorious when facing a formidable opponent like the IRS. I'd like to go into a bit more detail about each of the three strategies now.

Tax-Deferred Savings Strategies

This leg of my New Three-Legged Stool Approach to Financial Security is comprised of 401(k) accounts, traditional IRA accounts, annuities, and other employer-sponsored retirement plans. The main benefit of this leg is to help with income taxes while you're still working. It's the easiest money to save, because you're realizing an immediate tax benefit when you put money into one of these account types. Tax-deferred savings are also easier to invest in because the earnings are tax-deferred as well, so you can invest in these financial instruments that generate income without concerning yourself with an immediate tax liability.

Contributions to most employer-sponsored plans are made through payroll deductions, and most people never miss the money because it's automatically taken out of their net pay by their employers before they ever receive their paychecks. IRA contributions are also easy to make for those seeking a last-minute tax deduction before their filing deadline. For these reasons, tax-deferred savings are usually the largest portion of a person's savings. It's not unusual to see someone entering retirement with all of their financial assets in tax-deferred savings accounts.

The major problem with relying only on this scenario is that every dollar a retiree spends will be taxable when he or she reaches for it. For example, a retiree who wants to spend $100,000 from savings will need to withdraw $134,000 to net $100,000 after-tax. Note also tax law changes over the past several years have left many people ineligible to make a deductible IRA contribution. Those who are eligible can usually save a couple hundred dollars on their income taxes when making a contribution.

In addition, tax-deferred accounts come with penalties for drawing the money out before retirement age. Most employer plans will only allow early withdrawals in cases of extreme hardship or separation of employment.

After-Tax Savings Strategies

This leg is comprised of your bank and brokerage accounts, investment real estate—anything that isn't a tax-deferred retirement account. It's harder to save in these accounts because the money is taxed before you receive it. You must also be careful of how it's invested, because the investment return will be taxed along the way.

The benefit of after-tax savings doesn't come until you're already retired. When you want to spend $100,000 from your after-tax savings, there will be very little tax liability. What tax liability there is will most likely come from long-term capital gains, which currently has a maximum tax rate of 15% (20% for those in the highest tax bracket).

The biggest danger with after-tax savings isn't tax issues but accessibility. Because the money has already been taxed and there are usually no penalties to access it, it's the first place a person goes to get money. Funds originally earmarked for retirement can easily be spent on vacation homes, cars, college, and so forth. This is why many people end up with only tax-deferred savings at retirement: They've already spent the after-tax savings on other things along the way.

Tax-Free Savings Strategies

The final leg of the New Three-Legged Stool Approach includes accounts such as Roth IRAs and Roth 401(k)s. These account types have no immediate tax benefits. Instead, the real benefits come at retirement, because money withdrawn from a Roth IRA or Roth 401(k) after you turn age 59½ is tax-free. When you want to spend

$100,000 of your Roth IRA/401(k) money after you retire, you simply pull those funds from your Roth, and the tax liability is zero!

In light of this, you might wonder why everyone doesn't save for retirement in a Roth IRA/401(k). Unlike tax-deferred savings, Roth IRA/401(k)s offer no immediate tax benefits, so it's harder to save this way because it's done with after-tax dollars. A taxpayer left with the choice of putting money into a tax-deductible IRA or a Roth IRA will often choose the former because he or she will see an immediate return in tax savings.

The bigger problem for the Roth is getting money into it. The IRS limits who can contribute to a Roth IRA, based upon income. In 2016, a taxpayer can only contribute the maximum to a Roth if their modified adjusted gross income (MAGI) is less than $117,000 for a single filer or $184,000 for joint filers. In addition, Roth 401(k)s only started in 2006 and it took a few years before they caught on and employers started offering them.

————

The remainder of this book is dedicated to exploring each of these three critical topics in more detail, so you can enter retirement with a balanced Three-Legged Stool. In the next chapter, Leg One, we'll start our discussion of the first topic with a refresher course on the bread and butter of retirement plans: the tax-deferred savings account.

CHAPTER 1

Leg One: Tax-Deferred Savings Strategies

Tax-Deferred Accounts: A Refresher Course

The term *tax-deferred* refers to the postponement of paying taxes on earnings until a later date. There are many ways to defer taxes; rather than spend time on all of them, I'll focus this section on using retirement accounts for tax deferral.

Tax-deferred retirement accounts allow employees to save money in the present, dealing with taxes in the future. To take advantage of tax-deferred savings, an employee can choose to place pre-tax dollars, up to a certain amount, in various retirement accounts. These dollars aren't taxed when you place them in the account. They're only taxed when you withdraw them from the account.

RICK'S TIP: The best part about saving money in tax-deferred retirement accounts is you lower your current taxable income—and may be able to benefit from taxation at a lower tax bracket.

The two main types of retirement accounts are **individual** and **employer sponsored.** Let's take a closer look at these two types.

Individual Retirement Plans

Individual retirement plans are those that can be established without an employer. Primary examples include the individual retirement account (IRA) and solo 401(k). Two other types of individual accounts—Simplified Employee Pension (SEP) IRAs, and Savings Incentive Match Plan for Employees (SIMPLE) IRAs—may also function as employer sponsored plans. Details on each of these plans follow.

Individual Retirement Account (IRA)

An IRA is a personal retirement account that provides income tax advantages to individuals saving money for retirement. Because the objective of creating the IRA is to assist taxpayers in providing for their retirement, tax law levies penalties on withdrawals taken before retirement age of 59½. Tax law in the area of early withdrawals is complex. The typical tax penalty is 10% of the amount withdrawn prior to age 59½, unless certain exceptions apply. You should seek professional advice whenever you need to make significant withdrawals prior to age 59½, as many times you can avoid the penalty with proper planning. You usually must begin taking money from your IRA no later than April 1st of the calendar year following the date you reach age 70½. The rules established by the government regarding these required minimum distributions (RMDs), their timing, the amounts, the recalculations, and the effect various beneficiary designations have on them are among the most complex of the Internal Revenue Code. The penalty for failing to take timely withdrawals is 50% of the shortfall between what you should have withdrawn and the amounts you actually withdrew by the proper date. This punitive penalty is matched only by the civil fraud penalty in severity. The necessary calculations are therefore not something that most individuals should attempt on their own.

Contributions to IRAs

You can make deposits/contributions to an IRA each year up to the amounts allowable under the tax law. The contribution or deferred limits of an IRA plan are $5,500 in 2016. Employees age 50 or older can contribute another $1,000. An income tax deduction may be available for the tax year for which the funds are deposited. The principal and earnings on these deposits aren't taxed until you withdraw the money from the account. Withdrawals from an IRA may be subject to income taxation in the year in which you take them.

Solo 401(k)

A solo 401(k) plan works just like a regular 401(k) plan combined with a profit-sharing plan (see the next section for more on 401(k)s and profit-sharing plans). The difference is a solo 401(k) can only be implemented by self-employed individuals or small business owners who have no other full-time employees (the exception is if your full-time employee is your spouse). If you have any other full-time employees age 21 or older, or part-time employees who work more than 1,000 hours a year, you must include them in any plan you set up, which negates your ability to adopt a solo 401(k) plan.

Contributions to 401(k)s

In 2016, the contribution limit to solo 401(k)s is $18,000. An additional $6,000 may be contributed by employees age 50 or older.

Simplified Employee Pension Individual Retirement Account (SEP) IRAs

An SEP IRA is a type of retirement plan an employer with less than 25 employees can establish, including self-employed individuals with no employees. SEP IRAs are adopted by sole proprietors or small business owners to provide retirement benefits for themselves and, if they have some, their employees. Benefits of this approach are there are no significant administration costs for a self-employed person with no employees, and the employer is allowed a tax deduction for contributions made to the SEP plan. The employer makes contributions to each eligible employee's SEP IRA on a discretionary basis. If the self-employed person has employees, each must receive the same benefits under the plan. Because SEP accounts are treated as IRAs, funds can be invested the same way as any other IRA.

Contributions to SEP IRAs

SEP IRA contributions are treated as part of a profit-sharing plan. Contributions are tax deductible and the employer can contribute up to 25% of an employee's net compensation (net compensation is after the SEP contribution has been made). For 2016, only the employee's first $265,000 in gross compensation is subject to the employer's contribution, which results in a maximum contribution of $53,000 (indexed annually for inflation). Employers are not required to make annual contributions; however, if they choose to do so, all eligible employees must receive those contributions. Contributions may be made to the plan up until the date the employer's tax return is due for that year.

When a business is a sole proprietorship, the employee/owner both pays themselves wages and makes a SEP contribution that's limited to 25% of wages, which are profits minus SEP contribution. For a particular contribution rate (CR), the reduced rate is CR/(1+CR); for a 25% contribution rate, this yields a 20% reduced rate. Thus the overall contribution limit (barring limits) is 20% of 92.935225% (which equals 18.587045%) of net profit.

Participants can withdraw the money at age 59½. Prior to that, there is a 10% penalty or exercise tax. Distributions are taxable as ordinary income in the year they are received.

Savings Incentive Match Plan for Employees (SIMPLE) IRAs

The SIMPLE IRA is a type of employer-provided retirement plan available to an "eligible employer"—an employer with no more than 100 employees. An employer who has already established a SIMPLE IRA may continue to be eligible for two years after crossing the 100 employee limit. Self-employed workers with no employees are also eligible to establish these accounts.

The SIMPLE IRA is an attractive plan for employers because it doesn't incur many of the administrative fees and paperwork of plans such as the 401(k). Employers also benefit from the tax-deductible contributions to the plan. Employees may elect to establish salary deferrals to contribute to the plan like the 401(k). Assets inside SIMPLE IRAs can be invested like any other IRAs: in stocks, bonds, mutual funds, bank deposits, and so forth.

CONTRIBUTIONS TO SIMPLE IRAs

Like a 401(k) plan, the SIMPLE IRA is funded by a pre-tax salary reduction; and, like other salary reduction contributions, these deductions are subject to ordinary taxes including Social Security, Medicare, and federal unemployment tax (FUTA). Contribution limits for SIMPLE plans are lower than for most other types of employer-provided retirement plans: $12,500 for 2016, compared to $18,000 for conventional defined contribution plans. Employees age 50 or older can contribute an additional catch-up amount of $3,000.

With SIMPLE IRAs, the employer has the option of matching the employee's deferrals up to 3% of the annual salary or making non-elective contributions of 2% or less to all eligible employees. For 2016, the employer match is based on compensation up to a maximum of $265,000.

Although the employer may pick the financial institution in which to deposit the SIMPLE IRA funds, employees have the right to transfer the funds to another financial institution of their choice without cost or penalty. Distributions from SIMPLE IRAs follow the same rules as regular IRAs, with one exception: If premature distributions are taken before the employee reaches age 59½, and during the first two years after the employee starts participating in the plan, the penalty is 25%, not the usual 10%. Withdrawals are fully taxable at regular income tax rates and mandatory withdrawals must begin at age 70½. A SIMPLE IRA account can be rolled over into a traditional IRA tax-free after the first two years.

Employer-Sponsored Retirement Plans

Employer-sponsored accounts are only available to employees of the business offering them. Employer-sponsored plans fall into one of two categories: **defined benefit** or **defined contribution** plans. The most common type of defined benefit plan is the pension, and the most common type of defined contribution plans are the 401(k), 403(b), and 457 plans. The Simplified Employee Pension (SEP) IRAs and Savings Incentive Match Plan for Employees (SIMPLE) IRAs I described in the previous section may also fall under this category for employers with limited numbers of employees. Keep reading to find out more about these plan types.

Defined Benefit (Pension) Plans

A defined benefit plan is commonly referred to as a pension. A pension is a steady income given to a retiree, typically in the form of a guaranteed monthly annuity. The formula for calculating the amount of pension income a retiree will receive is usually based on a combination of service and salary. For example, a pension formula may state the employee earns 1.5% for each year worked (the service portion) times their average earnings for the last five years (salary portion). In this example, a retiree with average earnings of $100,000 and 30 years of service would receive a pension of $45,000 per year.

Defined Contribution Plans

A defined contribution plan provides an individual account for each participant. The benefit received by the retiree is based solely on the amount contributed to the account plus earnings on the funds invested. The contribution formula is usually based on salary only and could be a fixed percentage each year or varied depending on the profits of the company. When the company chooses to tie the amount of the contribution to its profits, the plan is referred to as a "profit-sharing" plan. When the contribution is based on a fixed percentage, it's called a "money purchase" plan. Upon retirement, the employee's account is used to provide retirement benefits, which can be paid in a variety of ways, such as through the purchase of an annuity, to provide a regular monthly income.

In the past few decades, defined contribution plans have grown rapidly and are now replacing traditional defined benefit plans as the primary retirement savings account for most employees. This change has shifted greater responsibility for retirement income from employers to individuals. Future benefits from these accounts depend on the level of contributions from the employee and employer during their careers. I spend some time below discussing the primary types of defined contributions plans:

401(K) PLANS

The most common type of defined contribution plan is the 401(k). Under section 401(k) of the Internal Revenue Code, enacted in 1978, employer and employee contributions to tax-deferred retirement accounts are excluded from wages subject to the federal income tax. Earnings within the accounts are tax deferred until they are withdrawn, when the money is taxed as ordinary income. In the Economic Growth and Tax Relief Reconciliation Act (EGTRRA) of 2001, Congress raised the maximum allowable contributions to defined contribution plans and proposals for further increases will likely remain on the legislative agenda. There are also restrictions on how and when employees can withdraw these assets, and penalties may apply if withdrawals are made while an employee is under the retirement age as defined by the plan.

In most 401(k) plans, the employee elects to have a portion of his or her wages paid directly, or deferred, into his or her 401(k) account. The employee can select from a number of investment options for the contributed funds. Most employers offer an assortment of mutual funds that emphasize stocks, bonds, money markets, or the company's stock.

Contributions to 401(k) Plans: The process for making contributions to 401(k) plans involves employees making periodic contributions from their paychecks before taxes. Any investment earnings or additional amounts matched by the company are also tax deferred until retirement. For 2016, the contribution or deferred limits of a 401(k) plan are $18,000. Employees age 50 or older can contribute an additional $6,000.

Employers that offer matching contributions usually base the amount on what the employee contributes. This matching contribution is often 25%, 50%, or even 100% up to a maximum level set by the employer. It's best for employees to contribute at least as much as the employer is willing to match to take advantage of this valuable employee benefit.

403(B) PLANS

The 403(b) is a tax-deferred retirement plan available to employees of educational institutions and certain non-profit organizations as determined by section 501(c)(3) of the Internal Revenue Code. The company determines further eligibility based on an employee's salary and status (for example, full-time versus part-time). The 403(b) plan has many of the same characteristics and benefits of a 401(k). Contributions can grow tax-deferred until withdrawal, at which time the money is taxed as ordinary income.

RICK'S TIP: One of the best features of the 401(k) plan is the match some employers will make to the employees' contributions. As a defined contribution plan, the amount the participant gets in retirement is based on the amount contributed to the plan and investment returns on those contributions.

Contributions to 403(b) Plans: The annual contribution limits for 403(b)s are the same as 401(k)s: $18,000 for 2016, and employees age 50 or older can contribute another $6,000. An additional catch-up provision may be available to employees age 50 or older. This increase is known as the 15-year-rule, a special provision that increases the elective deferral limit by as much as $3,000 more than the current $18,000 limit (as of 2016). To qualify, an employee must have completed at least 15 years of service with the same employer (years of service need not be consecutive) and can't have contributed more than an average of $5,000 to a 403(b) in previous years. The increase in the elective deferral limit can't exceed $3,000 per year under this provision, up to a $15,000 lifetime maximum.

Employees get to choose where their money is to be invested from among the plan providers offered by employers. The providers offer different investment options but employers aren't responsible for administrating the plans. 403(b) plan providers primarily offer annuities and some mutual funds. The annuities can be either fixed or variable. As with all annuities, gains aren't taxed until the participant starts receiving distributions.

457 PLANS

A 457 plan is a tax-exempt, deferred compensation program made available to employees of state and federal governments and agencies. The 457 plan is similar to a 401(k) plan, except there are never employer matching contributions and the IRS doesn't consider it a qualified retirement plan. Another key difference is there is no 10% penalty for withdrawal before the age of 59½. However, the withdrawal is subject to ordinary income taxation.

Participants can defer some of their annual income, and contributions and earnings are tax-deferred until withdrawal. Distributions start at retirement age but participants can also take distributions if they change jobs or in certain emergencies. Participants can choose to take distributions as a lump sum, annual installments, or an annuity. Distributions are subject to ordinary income taxes and the amounts can't be transferred into an IRA.

Contributions to 457 Plans: For 2016, an employee can contribute $18,000 into a 457 plan. The 457 plan allows for two types of catch-up provisions. The first is for employees over age 50, who can contribute a catch-up amount of $6,000 into their governmental 457 (catch-up contributions aren't provided for non-governmental 457 plans). The second, which is also available only to governmental 457 plans, is much more complicated and can be elected instead by an employee who is within three years of normal retirement age. This second catch-up option is equal to the full employee deferral limit, or another $18,000, for 2016. The second type of catch-up provision is limited to unused deferral limits from previous years. An employee who had deferred the maximum amount allowed into the 457 plan each year of employment previously wouldn't be able to utilize this extra catch-up.

Health Savings Accounts

Health savings accounts (HSAs) can play an important role in your retirement savings strategy. HSAs are actually a hybrid of two legs from the New Three-Legged Stool strategy of building a tax-efficient retirement portfolio. An HSA allows you to set aside tax-deductible dollars today to provide funds for health-related expenses. The tax-deductible component acts like Leg One of the stool. The funds within the account are withdrawn tax-free if they are used for qualified medical expenses, which acts like Leg Three of the stool.

> **RICK'S TIP:** Although governmental 457 plans may be rolled into other types of retirement plans, including IRAs, non-governmental 457 plans can only be rolled into another non-governmental 457 plan.

An HSA has some important advantages over other ways of saving for healthcare costs:

- Contributions are pre-tax. Contributions to an HSA are made before taxes are paid, like a traditional IRA or a 401(k) retirement plan. This makes it easier for a taxpayer to save because taxes aren't deducted before deposits are made to the HSA.
- Deposits can carry from year to year. HSA contributions roll over from one year to the next if they aren't needed for healthcare expenses. A flex spending account (FSA) must use all the money deposited each year or forfeit it. HSA funds can continue to build year after year if they aren't needed.

- Investment choices. Balances in an HSA can be invested in mutual funds and other financial instruments much like a 401(k). Investment options can help the account grow more quickly than in a traditional savings account.
- Tax-free withdrawals. Funds withdrawn from an HSA for approved medical expenses are not taxable. The pre-tax contributions and any earnings while the money was inside the account are tax-free when the funds are used for appropriate medical expenses. This makes an HSA an extremely efficient way to save money for health expenses when you have a high deductible health plan (HDHP).

HSAs are available to anyone with a qualified HDHP. Currently, the IRS defines a HDHP as one with annual deductibles between $1,300 and $6,450 for an individual plan ($2,600 and $12,900 for family plans). The deductible amounts are adjusted annually for inflation. Anyone, including employers and other family members, can pay into the account once established. Yearly contributions to HSAs are limited and the amount changes annually. The maximum contribution in 2016 for an individual is $3,350 ($6,750 for a family). There is a catch-up contribution of an additional $1,000 for taxpayers age 55 or older.

HSAs are not perfect. There are some drawbacks to be aware of before entering into this type of health coverage:

- HDHP requirement. The high deductible plan may not be comfortable for some people. Some may be reluctant to seek medical care because of the deductibles, especially when someone is just getting started with an HSA and funds have not been able to build inside the account. Some people will not be comfortable with an HDHP. They may be concerned about the taxes and penalties if the money was needed for another purpose.

- Taxes and penalties. HSA withdrawals for non-medical use are taxable and subject to penalties when the account owner is under age 65. The penalties disappear at age 65 but a non-medical use withdrawal is still subject to taxes.
- Contribution limits. In addition to the limits mentioned above, taxpayers over age 55 can make catch-up contributions of an additional $1,000 each year. Anyone who needs to set aside more than this for medical expenses will need to use a traditional savings account without the tax benefits.
- Investment limitations. HSA accounts must hold a minimum balance before account owners can invest. Typically a balance will need to remain in the account for potential medical expenses. Investment options are limited to the offerings of each plan much like a 401(k) account.

Withdrawals of funds from HSAs are only tax-free if used to pay for qualified medical expenses not covered by the HDHP. The definition of a qualified expense includes dental and vision expenses as well as chiropractic, acupuncture, and other forms of alternative treatments. Funds can also be withdrawn tax-free to pay for medical supplies and long-term care insurance. Withdrawals for any other reason are subject to a 20% penalty. The penalty is eliminated after you reach age 65.

After you reach age 65, your HSA is essentially an IRA account. You can withdraw funds for any reason without penalty. A withdrawal for any reason other than medical purposes will be subject to income tax.

There is a strategy for using your HSA like a Roth IRA. Make the maximum contribution each year and invest the funds. Save your medical expense receipts; don't submit them for reimbursement from the HSA. The funds will grow tax deferred inside the HSA and can be withdrawn tax-free in the future by submitting the old receipts for reimbursement. The strategy allows you to benefit from the long-term untaxed growth in the account.

An HSA is another important tool for those looking to build a tax-efficient retirement using the New Three-Legged Stool strategy. You should remember that an HDHP is required but these plans are not necessarily the best choice for your situation. Your general health and that of your family members is an important consideration.

Prevent the IRS From Touching Tax-Deferred Distributions

In the first part of Leg One, we talked about the primary types of tax-deferred savings strategies, which include IRAs, pensions, 401(k)s, and many other plans. One of the biggest decisions you'll face when you retire is how to start tapping into these plans. At that point, the money you've been saving tax-free throughout your career will finally be subjected to taxes. Your challenge will be to prevent the IRS from taking too much of your distributions in taxes.

There are three types of distribution options from employer-sponsored plans: **annuity, lump sum,** and **partial lump sum.** The Department of Labor requires that all plans must offer an annuity payment. However, not all plans are required to offer lump sum or partial lump sum. Hopefully your employer will allow you to choose among the three, though some employer plans only allow annuity payments. Let's examine each choice.

Annuity Payments

All employer plans are required to offer you an annuity payout in the form of monthly income. These payments will continue for the rest of your life. (In the case of your 401(k), you can surrender the balance to an insurance company that will guarantee payments for life with the amount of monthly payment depending on the balance in

RICK'S TIP: Alabama, Illinois, Mississippi, New Hampshire, Pennsylvania, and Tennessee don't tax pensions. Alaska, Florida, Nevada, South Dakota, Texas, Washington, and Wyoming have no state income tax. All other states may tax all or part of your pension income.

the account and your age.) When considering early retirement, the annuity payouts will be smaller, because you have a longer life expectancy. The payments are taxed as ordinary income and do not qualify for any special tax treatment for federal income tax purposes. Some states tax these payments, and others don't.

In most cases, annuity payments aren't eligible to be rolled over (transferred) to an IRA. Rolling over distributions from an employer plan to an IRA avoids taxation. The one exception is if the annuity payouts are for a period of less than 10 years. Note that a 10-year payout isn't less than 10 years. Read the following story of Mark Johnson, who learned this lesson the hard way.

CASE STUDY
Mark Johnson, retiree

Mark was a retiree who elected a 10-year payout of his pension, because the company he was retiring from didn't offer a lump sum distribution. He had been retired for three years when he started doing some consulting work. Because he didn't need the pension income, he put the payments into his IRA and called it a rollover. But the IRS doesn't allow these payouts to be rolled over, because the period elected wasn't less than 10 years.

Mark had to withdraw all of the contributions he had made and the earnings. The excess contributions were subject to a 15% penalty. His tax returns needed to be amended for the years he didn't claim the pension income, and he had to pay back taxes with interest. The

IRS could have charged a penalty for the back taxes but chose not to, because we caught the mistake and corrected it voluntarily. The mistake was costly enough as it was.

The moral of this story is: When you're asked to choose a payout option for your annuity upon retirement, choose wisely! With most retirement plans, this is an irrevocable decision.

Payout options vary among plans, but the following choices are the most frequently offered:

- Life Income. This option will provide an income for as long as you live; however, the pension dies with you. So although life income will give you the maximum monthly income available, there are no benefits available to your heirs.
- Joint and Last Survivor (J&LS). With this option, you'll receive a pension for life and provide a survivor income for the life of your spouse. This survivor income will usually represent a percentage of your pension income, typically anywhere from 50% to 100%. But remember your monthly pension will be reduced when you add a beneficiary. The greater the benefit to the beneficiary, the smaller the pension income will be to you.
- Life Income With Guarantee. This option will also provide you with an income for the rest of your life; however, if you die before the end of the guarantee period, the remaining payments in this period will be paid to your beneficiary. For example: If you died in the eighth year of a 20-year guarantee, 12 years of payments would be paid to your beneficiary. The guarantee periods generally range from five to 20 years. Note: Not all pensions have a guarantee clause; they must only offer the life or joint life options. The concern of some retirees is that

they elect the life option and then pass away after only receiving a few payments with nothing going to their heirs. The guarantee period is to assure that the heirs will receive something if the retiree passes away soon after beginning distributions.

- Joint and Last Survivor (J&LS) With Guarantee Period. With this option, you may add a guarantee like the one I described above to your J&LS pension. This is an important consideration if you and your spouse want to be sure there's money payable to your estate in the event of both of your premature deaths.

  Although there are a range of annuity payment options available, this approach still has flexibility problems. Let's say, for example, you choose the J&LS option. Your monthly payment is reduced to cover your spouse if you're the first to die. What happens if your spouse dies before you? You won't need the survivor protection anymore, but the payment won't revert to the higher amount. You'll be paying for a survivor benefit you no longer need for the rest of your life. Even if you were to remarry, you can't add your new spouse as beneficiary.

- Income Drawdown. This option is a variation on the other choices. Here, the pension administrator calculates the present value of what your payments will be over your life expectancy and shows this amount as a lump sum. Each time you receive a payment, this lump sum is reduced until it reaches zero. If you were to die before the lump sum is exhausted, the balance would be paid to your beneficiary.

Inflation creates another problem for most annuity payments in the private sector. Government pensions usually offer cost of living adjustments (COLA), though they're not always automatic. Retiring at age 65 with a $3,500 per month pension may be a comfortable income today, but that amount will have the purchasing power of only $1,900 per month in 20 years at an inflation rate of just 3.0%. Your standard of living would erode significantly if you didn't have any other savings to supplement your income.

Finally, when you submit your pension paperwork, you're making a decision that hopefully will need to last 20 to 30 years. Are you ready to make that kind of decision when you retire? I can't tell you how many clients have sat in my office at retirement and said, "Rick, I'm finally retired, and I'm not going to work another day in my life!" Yet a year later, many of those same people say, "Rick, I'm sick and tired of doing chores around the house. I need something to keep my mind occupied. I've decided to do some consulting work for my former employer a couple days a week." Those people no longer need the same pension income, but they can't turn it off, and they end up paying tax on it every year because the payments aren't eligible for rollover.

Lump Sum Payments

If you decide to take a lump sum distribution of your entire balance from all of your employer's qualified plans (pension, profit-sharing, or stock bonus plans), you have one year from the date of your retirement to complete the transaction.

Once you indicate your choice, you'll be asked whether or not you plan to roll it over to an IRA. If you choose not to roll it over to an IRA, the employer is required to withhold 20% for taxes. All of the investment earnings and pre-tax contributions will be subject to income tax. You'll also be subject to a 10% early withdrawal penalty if you aren't age 55 or older.

There are several advantages to choosing a lump sum payout. Rolling it over directly to an IRA avoids the 20% withholding and allows the money to continue to grow tax deferred until you decide to draw it out. You can roll it over to an IRA and then start taking monthly distributions. If you use the inflation-fighting investments

I describe in Leg Two (see Chapter 2), you can increase that amount each year to keep pace with inflation. The payments can be stopped or modified if you decide to do some consulting work.

You can also take a lump sum amount if you want to make a down payment on a vacation home or other big purchase. Your IRA allows you to name a beneficiary who'll receive the balance in the account when you die. You can name multiple beneficiaries and change them whenever you want. Finally, if you decide later you'd rather have a guaranteed monthly income, you can use the lump sum from your IRA to buy an annuity with the balance in your account.

If your employer offers both after-tax and pre-tax retirement options, you'll be glad to know the EGTRRA I described earlier liberalized the rules regarding the permissible movement (portability) of assets between eligible retirement plans. The changes to these rules now allow you to roll over after-tax assets from your company plan to your IRA.

The benefit of rolling over the after-tax assets is the earnings continue to grow tax-deferred in your IRA. The drawback is you'll be responsible for keeping track of the after-tax assets in your IRA by filing a form 8606 with your tax return each year you make contributions or withdrawals. This may be desirable if you're going to implement the Roth strategy I describe in Leg Three (see Chapter 3). If not, you'll want to elect to receive the after-tax contributions in a separate check so they aren't commingled in your IRA.

The IRS issued a ruling in 2014 providing a path for rolling over any after-tax money in an employer-sponsored plan directly to a Roth IRA. Employees with after-tax money in these plans can take a complete distribution and direct the plan administrator to send pre-tax dollars to a traditional IRA or another plan, and then roll the after-tax contributions into a Roth IRA tax-free. (Read more about this recent ruling in Leg Three.)

If you're holding any money in your retirement account in company stock, you'll need to elect how that money is to be distributed.

RICK'S TIP: Many employers that offer both pre-tax and after-tax retirement options commingle the two in one overall retirement plan statement. The administrator for your qualified plan is ultimately responsible for keeping track of which portion of your balance is attributed to after-tax and pre-tax assets. However, it helps if you check your statements periodically to ensure the tabulations match what you think they should be. This will allow you to clarify possible discrepancies with the plan administrator.

(See the section titled "NUAs Prevent the IRS From Pilfering Retirement Fund Deposits" for a full discussion on this topic.)

Let's look at the two options side by side on page 45.

As you can see, when given the option of either an annuity or a lump sum payout, it's important to know the pros and cons of each. Many retirees choose the latter for its overall flexibility and advantages.

Partial Lump Sum (PLS) Payments

Some public employee pension plans offer retirees a combination of lump sum and annuity payments, which is generally referred to as a partial lump sum (PLS) option. This option allows retirees to receive a portion of their retirement benefit as a one-time payment in exchange for a permanently reduced monthly annuity payment. The PLS payment will reduce the account balance used to calculate the annuity payment dollar for dollar. Reducing the account balance by taking a PLS won't affect the length of time the monthly annuity benefit is payable.

Most plans require the PLS to be between defined minimum and maximum amounts. For example, the plan may stipulate the payment can't be less than six times or more than 36 times the monthly amount that would be payable under the plan of payment selected.

Annuity	Lump Sum
Monthly payment guaranteed. Must take along with the tax burden whether you need it or not. Annuity payments are considered ordinary income, subject to federal income tax but not state income tax in PA. You will have that monthly income as long as you live.	*No exact payment guaranteed or required.* When rolled to an IRA can be flexible about distributions and the tax burden that accompanies them. Distributions without penalty can be taken at age 59 1/2 but can be deferred until age 70 1/2. Distributions are ordinary income, subject to federal income tax but not state income tax in PA.
Not subject to market risk. No investment required. No investment fees.	*Subject to market risk.* You are going to have to invest the lump sum in an IRA and manage it, either on your own or with assistance. You will pay some investment management fees.
No cost of living increases. Over time the purchasing power of the static monthly amount will erode.	*More protection from inflation.* It is possible for your investment to keep pace and exceed inflation with stock market exposure.
No benefit to your heirs. The monthly stream stops when you die unless you are eligible for and select a Joint and Survivor annuity at a reduced monthly amount.	*Benefits your heirs.* If you die before spending all your IRA assets, you can leave them to a beneficiary. The assets get rolled over to a beneficiary IRA and can be used for that person's retirement or when needed. Only a small annual distribution is required.

The maximum amount could also be worded in a way that the lump sum payment can't result in a monthly benefit that's less than 50% of the original monthly benefit. The total amount paid as lump sum and monthly payments will be equal to the amount that would have been paid had the retiree not elected to receive a lump-sum payment.

As a lump-sum distribution, the PLS is fully taxable and subject to the other rules connected to a full lump-sum distribution.

Tax Alternatives to the IRA Rollover

In the previous sections, we talked about the benefits of rolling over your retirement account distributions to an IRA. Although doing this will allow you to avoid the tax man for a while longer, you may be interested in exploring other options that force you to pay the IRS piper up-front but could be better suited to your situation. These options include:

- **Ten-Year Averaging.** In order to qualify for 10-year averaging, you must meet the following criteria:
    - If you have more than one account in any category, all of the accounts must be distributed as a lump sum distribution in a single tax year.
    - You can't have previously used 10-year averaging for figuring tax on a lump sum distribution.
    - You participated in the plan for at least five years prior to the tax year of lump sum distribution.
    - The plan was a tax qualified plan under the tax law.
    - You were born before January 1, 1936.

    If you meet the above tax tests, the lump sum distribution you report on your tax return may qualify for special tax treatment that includes the 10-year averaging tax option. This doesn't mean you get to pay one-tenth of the tax each year for the next 10 years. Rather, you pay the entire tax in one year, but the tax is calculated as if the distribution had been received over 10 years. If you want to consider this option, be sure to consult a tax professional who's experienced with this calculation to help you through the process.

- **Capital Gains.** The 20% capital gains tax election can be made to compute the tax on the taxable part of the lump sum distribution that applies to the portion received for participating in the plan before 1974. This choice allows taxpayers who were born before 1936 to have the pre-1974 taxable portion taxed at a 20% tax rate, and the rest of the lump sum distribution, including the portion for all post-1974 participation, taxed as ordinary income using the 10-year averaging tax option.

- **Ordinary Income.** A lump sum (and PLS) distribution will be subject to ordinary income tax in the year you receive it. Payments made to a retiring employee directly from an employer plan are subject to the mandatory withholding of 20% federal tax, but this doesn't necessarily mean it's taxed at 20%. If you receive a large distribution in one tax year, it could easily put you in the highest tax bracket of 39.6%.

Let's look at some case studies to explore the thought process that goes into deciding which distribution method is best in a given

RICK'S TIP: When it finally comes time to choose from among these options upon your retirement, your employer should provide you with a form called a "Request for Distribution" election form that lists each choice. Completing this form correctly is a critical step in the retirement process. Making a mistake can be costly in the form of taxes and/or lost opportunity costs while the mistake is corrected.

situation. I want to stress how important it is to think through these options and get counsel before making your election. You only have one chance to make these elections, and the implications are significant. I have people coming into my office all the time with a retirement mess, and I ask them why they made the choices they did. Many times, I find they just followed what someone else had done who had retired before them. Yet the circumstances of each retiree are unique. You want to make the right choice for you, and that choice may be something completely different than what a coworker did.

CASE STUDY
Jonas Beiler, former military officer and retiree

Jonas Beiler had several careers during his working lifetime and was preparing to retire from a company he'd worked with for the past 10 years. Jonas retired earlier from the military and was already receiving a pension from the Navy. He'd accumulated $300,000 in his 401(k) and wanted to take it as a lump sum and use the proceeds to pay off the mortgage on a property he bought a few years earlier in Florida. He and his wife, Sarah, planned to split their time between Pennsylvania and Florida during their retirement. The Beilers came to me for help with figuring out how to meet these goals.

We determined between Jonas's Navy pension, Social Security, and the couple's other savings, they wouldn't need this $300,000 to meet future income needs. Jonas was born before January 1, 1936, so he qualified for 10-year averaging. The money had all been put into the account in the last 10 years, so none of it was eligible for capital gains treatment. Jonas could take the money out as a lump sum and pay ordinary income tax on the distribution, or he could apply 10-year averaging. Let's look at the difference between the two options:

Ordinary income tax: $100,770
Ten-year averaging: $64,475

The other option was to try to spread the distribution over more than one tax year. That would disqualify the distribution for 10-year averaging treatment. The tax under 10-year averaging treatment was so favorable it made for an easy decision.

CASE STUDY

Victor Goldman, consultant and retiree

Victor was age 55 and was leaving his current position to start a consulting business on his own. He already had clients who wanted to use his services, and he estimated he'd be able to comfortably provide for his income needs from his consulting income for 10 years into the future. His 401(k) was worth $500,000, and he sought my advice about whether he should take it as a lump sum and pay the tax right then, as he was 55 and not subject to a 10% penalty, or if he should roll over the money to an IRA and pay the tax later.

Victor's options:

Direct Transfer Rollover @ 8% Return
$500,000 grows to $1,079,460 in 10 years
4% prudent withdrawal = $43,175 per year ($34,540 after-tax)

Lump Sum Distribution With 20% Withheld for Tax
$400,000 grows to $743,830 in 10 years @ 6.4% after-tax
4% prudent withdrawal = $29,750 per year after-tax

Income tax rates would have had to increase dramatically in the next 10 years for the strategy to favor taking the lump sum right then. Even if Victor had qualified for 10-year averaging, paying the tax right then provided a significant disadvantage he probably wouldn't have been able to overcome within a 10-year time frame. Because he didn't need to use all the money at the time, he elected the direct transfer rollover.

CASE STUDY

Dave Mills, engineer

Dave was a former engineer who always prided himself on thoroughly researching a topic and making informed decisions. When he retired from a local farm equipment company, he decided to make all his retirement decisions on his own, as he'd always done his own investing and had grown his 401(k) to $1 million. Unfortunately, he made a $200,000 mistake simply by failing to check the right box on his Request for Distribution form.

By neglecting to check the rollover box, Dave's employer thought his retirement money was coming directly out of its plan, making it subject to the 20% mandatory withholding. So, Dave's employer withheld 20% for taxes and sent him a check for the difference. Dave called his employer immediately after he received the check, but it was too late: The employer had already sent the $200,000 to the IRS, because employers are required to submit taxes withheld within 24 hours if the amount exceeds $100,000. The IRS literally got its money before Dave did, and Dave then called me seeking help on how to fix his mistake.

Dave could have simply rolled the remaining $800,000 over to an IRA and been done with it. But look at the consequences of that choice:

Distribution Amount	$1,000,000
20% Withholding	($200,000)
	=======
Net Check Received	$800,000
Tax on $200,000	($50,000)
Penalty if under age 55	($20,000)
Lost earnings on $200,000	($12,000)
Total Shrinkage	($82,000)

Another alternative would've been for Dave to come up with $200,000 from his personal funds so he could roll the whole $1 million over to the IRA. But not many people have an extra $200,000 lying around, including Dave. However, he did have a home worth $500,000 that had a mortgage balance of $100,000.

We arranged for a home equity line of credit (LOC). Dave borrowed $200,000 from the LOC and subsequently rolled over the entire $1 million within the 60-day limit required for such transactions. When he filed his taxes the following year, he recouped the $200,000 that was withheld and paid back the line of credit. He had to pay the bank interest on the $200,000 he borrowed—but the IRS didn't pay Dave a dime on his $200,000 they held onto for a year.

To avoid making Dave's mistake yourself, you can elect a direct rollover to an IRA. The direct rollover won't be subject to 20% mandatory withholding. The rollover will still be reported to the IRS as a distribution, but will be coded as a rollover on the 1099-R, a tax reporting document similar to the 1099-DIV brokerage firms use to report dividend income. You'll need to show the amount on your tax return for the year the money was distributed, but, as a rollover, it won't be taxed.

RICK'S TIP: If you aren't sure how to fill out the rollover paperwork, by all means, get help! In order for a distribution to be a direct rollover, the proceeds must be made payable to the custodian for the benefit of the employee. Sometimes the check goes directly to the custodian. Other employer plans make the check payable to the custodian but send it to the employee. Either way is acceptable. But beware: If you receive your check and it's 20% light, you made a mistake, and the 60-day clock is ticking! You'll only have 60 days to figure out a way to make the best of the situation.

You should also be careful if you're rolling over company stock. You'll want to read the next section on NUAs to determine if you want to roll over the stock or take it in kind. If you decide to roll over the stock to an IRA, make sure you're dealing with a custodian that can accept stock. I highly recommend you consult with a financial adviser who's experienced with handling rollovers with company stock. The tax laws involving company stock rollovers are very complicated; I typically see a 50% error rate with rollovers involving company stock in some form. Most of the mistakes can't be fixed, and the tax consequences are high.

For example, I've seen cases where the employee took the company stock out of the plan and replaced it with cash so he could say the entire amount was rolled over. This isn't permitted! The consequences involve an excess contribution penalty on the cash contribution. The cash contribution must be removed from the IRA and tax paid on any earnings as well as on the stock distribution. The stock distribution will also be subject to penalty for not being reported as a taxable distribution.

Dave may also have been able to avoid his mistake if he'd simply left his retirement in his 401(k) plan, which some employers allow. There are good reasons to consider doing this. If you're not retiring but rather are going to work for another employer that has a 401(k), it's possible your new employer allows rollovers from other plans— so you could roll the money from your old plan directly into the new employer's plan. And, if you're between the ages 55 and 59½, withdrawals from an employer plan aren't subject to the same 10% IRS penalty you'd incur if you withdrew your money from an IRA during that same period. You must wait until age 59½ to withdraw penalty-free from an IRA.

On the other hand, the main problem with leaving the money in your employer's plan is the employer has control over it. It's your money, but the plan administrator has to sign off on distributions. What would happen if the employer went out of business? Another one of my clients, Marie Hawgood, found out.

CASE STUDY

Marie Hawgood, executive

Marie worked for a small company in Massachusetts that had a 401(k) plan with T. Rowe Price mutual funds. When she left the company to move to Pennsylvania, she left her 401(k) in place because she liked the T. Rowe Price funds and didn't need the money. The account was small, and over the years, she received quarterly statements indicating the funds were performing well. She made periodic changes online among the funds that were offered through the plan and was able to grow the account to $100,000 by the time she was ready to retire.

When Marie eventually tried to roll over the account to her IRA, she found she needed the administrator's signature to distribute the account—yet the company she had worked for was no longer in business. She came to me for help after six frustrating months of trying to get T. Rowe Price to release her own money. They weren't disputing the fact the funds belonged to Marie; instead, they were stating she didn't have the authority to distribute them.

We obtained a copy of the plan documents and were eventually able to track down one of the signers of the plan at his new job. Once the forms were properly signed, T. Rowe Price released the funds, and Marie rolled them over to her IRA. This was difficult enough with Marie on hand to help. I've helped with even more complex situations where the account owner was deceased, and we had to try to get the funds released to the beneficiary. In at least one instance, the dispute took two years to resolve. By then, we'd missed the deadline for electing distributions over the beneficiary's lifetime and were forced to distribute the account. The moral of this story: When in doubt, roll over your company plan to an IRA where you're in control of the funds!

CASE STUDY
Harry Thompson, retiree

The cost of mistakes aren't always tax related, as another one of my clients, Harry Thompson, discovered. Harry had been employed at Armstrong World Industries for more than 30 years. He retired with a good pension and had accumulated $800,000 in the company's 401(k) plan, $500,000 of which was in Armstrong stock. Armstrong stock had had a pretty good run and was trading at around $80 per share. Harry thought the stock should soon reach a high and wanted to be able to sell it quickly. He didn't like the method used to sell the stock when it was in the 401(k), so he decided to roll it over to an IRA so he'd have more control. He'd recently received a flyer from his insurance agent that said the agent could handle IRA rollovers, so he rolled over his whole 401(k) to an annuity through the agent.

What this agent (who'd never done a rollover involving stock) failed to tell Harry was that an annuity can't accept stock. Any stock would need to be sold before attempting the rollover. When Harry's first post-rollover statement arrived in the mail, it showed the $300,000 in non-stock deposits but the $500,000 in Armstrong stock didn't show anywhere, despite the fact his last 401(k) statement showed everything leaving the account. In the meantime, Armstrong stock hit $90 per share and then started coming down. After months of getting the run around from the insurance company about the whereabouts of the stock, Harry came to me in frustration to get the rollover completed.

We tried to get the rollover reversed, but the annuity had a 7% penalty on the $300,000, and the "free look" period had already passed. This meant the $300,000 had to stay put with the insurance company, or else the company would help itself to a $21,000 penalty. We finally tracked the stock down through the transfer agent. It had been registered to the insurance company as custodian for Harry's IRA. Once we knew where the certificate was, it was a simple matter to get the shares reissued. We set up an IRA account with a discount broker and had the shares reissued to the discount broker as custodian for Harry. Harry ended up with two IRAs: one with the insurance company and another with a discount broker for his company stock. They were both reported as rollovers, so there were no tax problems to deal with. The problem was the Armstrong stock had fallen to $50 per share, and the account was now worth $300,000. Harry had missed his opportunity to get out of the stock when it was trading at $90 per share.

Another detail of Harry's situation is he had a pension from Armstrong that wasn't eligible for rollover. He needed to decide whether to take a survivor benefit for his wife, Jean. Jean didn't have a pension of her own and, after evaluating their other resources, we determined Harry needed to provide a survivor benefit. The annuity would pay $3,000 per month with no benefit or $2,500 per month with a 50% survivor benefit. If Harry were to die, Jean would receive $1,250 per month.

Harry was 59 years old and in good health. We were able to find a life insurance company that would write a policy on Harry's life that would pay Jean $2,500 per month if Harry were to die. The premium on this policy was $450 per month. After qualifying for the policy and the stated premium, Harry elected the $3,000 per month pension with no survivor benefit. He used $450 of the pension income to pay the premium, which left him with a net income of $2,550 per month.

New Rule for IRA Rollovers

In 2014, a U.S. Tax Court's ruling[1] on IRA rollovers held that the one IRA rollover per year rule applies to all the IRA accounts of a taxpayer collectively—not to each IRA account individually. This ruling is contrary to the long-standing interpretation of IRS Publication 590's statement to the contrary.

The Internal Revenue Code allows taxpayers to take a distribution from an IRA and avoid tax consequences by rolling the funds over to an IRA within 60 days. The tax code permits one IRA rollover

RICK'S TIP: The strategy I referenced in the last paragraph of my case study about Harry Thompson is called pension maximization. I've found this strategy only works in about half of cases—mainly because most people aren't in good enough health at retirement to qualify for preferred rates. However, it's great when it works, because it addresses the problem of Jean passing away first. In this case, Harry could let the policy expire, because he would no longer need it. Or, if he remarried, he could change the beneficiary to his new wife so she'd be covered. This would not have been an option with the pension. In Harry's case, both he and Jean had more income than by taking the 50% survivor option.

in a 12-month period. Prior to the Tax Court's ruling, the one rollover per year rule was interpreted to apply to IRAs on an account-by-account basis. A taxpayer with several IRA accounts could take a 60-day rollover from each account, allowing multiple IRA rollovers in a 12-month period. The new ruling applies the once-per-year IRA rollover rule in the aggregate across all IRAs, invalidating the separate IRA rollover treatment.

This ruling has no impact on direct transfers between IRA accounts or rollovers from an employer's plan to an IRA. In these transactions, the taxpayer never touches the money. A trustee-to-trustee transfer is the best way for IRA money to be moved from one IRA to another. The money goes directly from one IRA custodian to another. There is no 60-day deadline and the once-per-year rule does not apply. IRA owners may continue to make as many direct transfers as they like.

The ruling has no impact on Roth conversions. When funds are converted from an IRA or employer plan (401(k), 403(b), and so on) to a Roth IRA, indirectly using the 60-day rollover, the conversion does not count as a rollover for purposes of the once-per-year rule. IRA re-characterizations are also not affected by the ruling.

The tax consequences of not following the new ruling can be severe. Attempting to make more than one IRA-to-IRA or Roth IRA–to–Roth IRA rollover within a 12-month period will result in the second distribution being considered a taxable distribution. The 10% penalty for early distributions will apply if the taxpayer is under age 59½ when the transaction occurs. Although the IRS has the authority to waive the 60-day rollover rule, it may not waive the once-per-year IRA-to-IRA rollover rule. Finally, the funds from the second distribution will become subject to the 6% excess contribution penalty if the taxpayer allows them to remain within an IRA. The 6% penalty will apply to each year the excess remains in the IRA account.

The bottom line from the new ruling is that any rollover from any IRA cancels the opportunity for any other IRA rollovers within a 12-month period. This period starts on the date the first distribution occurs from the first IRA. If an IRA rollover occurs from one IRA, the taxpayer cannot do another rollover from that IRA or a different one until the 12-month period is past.

The IRS acknowledged that this ruling is a significant departure from the standard view of IRS Publication 590's rollover limitation. The IRS began applying the rule to any rollover that involves an IRA distribution after January 1, 2015.

This rule is a potentially costly tax trap. Taxpayers should do a direct trustee-to-trustee transfer when moving funds between IRAs. This type of transfer is not considered a rollover and therefore not subject to the once-per-year problems. If you must do a rollover, pay close attention to the transaction date to make sure the 12-month period has passed before attempting another rollover.

Penalties

From the previous case studies, it's clear you should avoid expensive consequences of improperly handling your retirement assets. Having to pay income taxes on withdrawals is bad enough without also incurring penalties. Some of these penalties are well known; others aren't. Let's review some of the common transactions and mistakes that could result in IRS penalties on your IRA assets or IRA-related transactions.

Early-Distribution Penalty

If you are under age 59½ when a distribution occurs from your IRA, you may have to pay a 10% early-distribution penalty on the gross distribution amount. There are several exceptions to the 10% early-distribution penalty that are discussed throughout this book, primarily in the upcoming section on early retirement. Qualifying for one of these (or any other) exceptions can often be handled properly when the IRA custodian/trustee reports the distribution as one that meets an exception. Improper reporting could result in the need for you to pay penalties you may have avoided.

The IRS identified nearly 639,000 taxpayers (IRA values of $40.4 billion) in tax year 2012 with IRAs who may not have taken RMDs. There were also nearly 6,500 taxpayers who admitted they did not take RMDs in prior years. The tax on the missed RMDs totaled $6.2 million. The penalty on the missed distributions is calculated as 50% of the amount that should have been withdrawn. In total 335 of these taxpayers were able to get the penalty waived in full. The report stated that if a taxpayer fails to take their RMD by the December 31st deadline, the sooner they report the error and ask for a waiver, the more likely the IRS is to waive the 50% penalty.

The IRS has access to date of birth information from the Social Security Administration and is aware of which taxpayers are turning 70 ½ or older. IRA custodians are required to report year-end account values of IRAs on Form 5498. This form contains a checked box if the account owner is required to take a distribution that year. IRS Publication 590 says: "An RMD may be required even if the box is not checked." Taxpayers who deliberately avoid taking distributions thinking the IRS won't find out are mistaken. Ferreting out missed

RMDs is low-hanging fruit for the IRS and can easily be discovered by computer cross referencing.

Tax on Excess Contributions

Each year, there is a maximum limit on the amount you may contribute to an IRA. In 2016 the limit is $5,500, or $6,500 if you're age 50 or older. Contributions in excess of the limit are referred to as "excess contributions," and they must be removed plus any earnings by your tax-filing deadline (including extensions) for the year. Failure to do so will result in a 6% tax assessment on the excess amount for each year the excess remains in the IRA. The excess tax applies to any amount contributed to an IRA that shouldn't be, such as the examples above with the retiree who attempted to roll over his pension payments or the person trying to withdraw company stock and replacing it with cash. This excess tax penalty can become a substantial amount, and failure to remove the excess amount in a timely manner could result in double taxation of the assets.

Excess-Accumulation Tax

IRA owners must begin taking required minimum distributions (RMDs) from their IRAs for the year they reach age 70½, and they must continue to distribute a minimum amount from the IRA each subsequent year. There's a 50% penalty for failing to distribute the RMD amount. For example, if your RMD for last year was $10,000 and you distributed only $5,000 from your IRA, you'll owe the IRS $2,500 (50% of $5,000) plus tax on the entire $10,000.

NUAs Keep the IRS Away From Tax-Deferred Stock Distributions

I want to begin this section with a story about a client of mine, Rodney Hartwell, whose stock distributions from his tax-deferred retirement plan weren't structured in the most tax-efficient way possible.

Preserve Tax-Deferred Distributions:

- All employers are required to offer an annuity option for distributing your company retirement, but not all require you to take it. Elect the lump sum when offered. You can always convert the lump sum to annuity payments on your own at a later time.

- Be careful when electing your distribution using the company forms. Mistakes can result in lost investment earnings and significant tax penalties. Consult a retirement planner to help you evaluate which options are best for you and complete the paperwork properly.

- If you do make a mistake with your retirement distribution, get help quickly. There's only a 60-day window to fix rollover mistakes.

- Consult a retirement planner who's experienced with handling company stock in a retirement plan. Mistakes are costly and you don't want to miss an opportunity that may have been available to you.

- You may not always have been able to avoid paying income taxes, but you can avoid paying penalties. You don't want to suffer avoidable penalties and taxation on any retirement transactions. Make sure you are familiar with the various restrictions on contributions and distributions. Be sure to consult your tax professional regarding transactions that could result in penalties.

- Your coworker may know more than you do about financial matters, but his choices aren't necessarily the best ones to make for everyone. Consider your distribution options carefully in light of your own unique situation.

CASE STUDY

Rodney Hartwell, medical supply executive

Rodney Hartwell, an executive at a medical supply company, was planning on retiring at year-end. Rodney had $100,000 worth of employer's stock held in the company's 401(k) plan with a cost basis of $20,000. A local investment adviser recommended Rodney roll his company stock into a low-cost IRA, explaining the advantages of the IRA and telling Rodney his account would grow larger because the tax would be deferred—and there was also the likelihood of potential returns with the hot mutual fund he just happened to be recommending for the IRA.

The advice this investment adviser gave to Rodney wasn't unusual; tax-deferred savings accounts are most people's go-to method of saving for retirement. But as I mentioned in the last section, the major problem with this scenario is every dollar a retiree wants to spend is going to be taxable when he or she reaches for it.

The adviser likely failed to explain this unfortunate fact to Rodney, so when his IRA eventually began to distribute income, that income was taxed at ordinary income rates on his $20,000 cost basis and could eventually have been taxed even higher (35%) on his $80,000 gain.

The adviser could have recommended Rodney use an often-overlooked tax strategy known as net unrealized appreciation (NUA). How does an NUA work? Here's an example. An employee is about to retire and qualifies for a lump sum distribution from a qualified retirement plan. He elects to use the NUA strategy, receives the stock, and pays ordinary income tax on the average cost basis, which represents the original cost of the shares. This strategy allows the tax to be deferred on any appreciation that accrues from the time the stock is distributed until it's finally sold.

The NUA strategy would've allowed Rodney to receive an in-kind distribution of his company's stock and pay income tax only on the average cost basis of the shares, rather than on the current market value. In that case, Hartwell's tax on the $80,000 gain would be treated as long-term capital gains and taxed at a maximum of 15%, resulting in a potential tax savings of $12,000. (The $20,000 basis would be taxed as ordinary income.)

5 Steps to a Successful NUA Transaction

Before exercising a distributon or rollover, follow these five steps designed to help you understand what it takes to complete a successful NUA transaction.

1. **Start early.** The NUA transaction may take several weeks. Be sure to obtain a written copy of your cost basis before initiating the rollover. You can get the formal documentation of the cost basis of the company stock; you can also request formal documentation showing your employer's promise to make an in-kind distribution of the company shares.

2. **Determine the amount of gain in the stock price.** In an employer-sponsored retirement plan, you can elect an NUA on some, all, or none of the shares. Note, however, that on shares you bought for more than the current stock price, it's not logical to elect this strategy. Instead, seek out shares that are currently selling for twice your cost basis.

3. **Consider the sequence of transactions when the plan holds assets in addition to employer securities.** You can transfer the company stock portion (which still qualifies

RICK'S TIP: The NUA distribution must be taken as a lump sum distribution, not a partial lump sum distribution, and in order to qualify for a lump sum distribution, the employee must take the distribution all within the same calendar year.

for the tax break on the NUA) to a taxable (non-IRA) brokerage account, and you can roll the non-company stock portion of the plan into an IRA rollover account. You should execute the IRA rollover first for all assets except the company stock, then the NUA shares can be distributed in-kind, with nothing to withhold for the IRS from either transaction. Note that unless it's a trustee-to-trustee transfer, or the only remaining asset being distributed is employer stock, your employer should withhold 20% of distributions from a qualified plan for taxes.

4. **Know your liabilities.** Have your tax professional prepare a tax projection to determine the amount needed, and be prepared to pay the tax man in April.

5. **Prepare an exit strategy.** Assuming you're optimistic about the company's future and proceed with the in-kind distribution, you should still have an exit strategy if the stock starts to decline. One possibility would be to give

RICK'S TIP: A few words of caution before you jump on the NUA bandwagon: First, an NUA distribution may not be a good idea if the company's outlook is bleak. The tax benefits are wasted if the company stock declines significantly after the distribution. An investor with 98% of his retirement account tied up in one stock may want to consider liquidating a portion of his stock position and distributing a smaller portion of the stock in-kind. Second, never ask for in-kind distributions of company stock in December. It's better to wait until the beginning of the next year, because the entire distribution (rollover and in-kind distribution) must be completed in the same calendar year.

some or all of the stock to a charitable remainder uni-trust (CRUT). Once the stock is transferred to a CRUT, the shares can be sold by the trustee and reinvested in a diversified portfolio that can provide lifelong income to the donor. The charitable deduction might even offset most of the tax obligation on the cost basis.

Net Unrealized Appreciation

- If you own large quantities of company stock inside a retirement plan, you should know about net unrealized appreciation (NUA).
- NUA allows the tax to be deferred on any appreciation that accrues from the time the stock is distributed until it's finally sold.
- Distributions must be taken as lump sum distributions, not partial lump sum distributions.
- In order to qualify for the NUA treatment, an employee must complete the entire distribution within the same calendar year.

With the tax-deferred savings strategies I've covered in Leg One now under your belt, you can get started on creating the all-important tax-deferred part of your retirement savings plan. However, don't forget a well-rounded retirement plan includes more than just tax-deferred strategies; it must also include after-tax strategies, which I'll tell you about in greater detail in Leg Two (Chapter 2).

Leg Two: After-Tax Savings Strategies

Transfer Highly Taxed Assets Into Tax-Deferred Accounts

Remember: The after-tax savings strategies leg of my New Three-Legged Stool approach is made up of your bank and brokerage accounts, investment real estate—basically, anything that's not a tax-deferred retirement account. After-tax savings strategies have become more prevalent in the face of the growing recognition that we don't live in a tax-free environment.

As a result, we've had to recraft our tools in order to devise innovative new strategies that can keep our retirement assets from excessive taxation. For example, I've found that, for typical mutual funds on an after-tax basis, turnover was the real killer. That's why I use asset classes for my clients and lengthen the holding period, allowing growth on a compounding basis, then I reinvest the earnings. If you do this, your money will grow at a faster rate. Remember: It's not how much you earn, it's how much you keep!

To help illustrate the importance of including after-tax strategies in your retirement plan, I want to tell you a story about another retiree, Shirley Bachman.

CASE STUDY

Shirley Bachman, retiree

Shirley Bachman was a widow who had accumulated what she thought would be a comfortable savings for retirement. Her financial assets totaled $1 million, and was split nearly equally between an IRA and a taxable account. She counted on the income from her investment accounts, Social Security, and a small pension to make ends meet.

When Shirley turned 70½, she had to begin to take her required minimum distribution (RMD) from her IRA, and the additional taxable income was making 85% of her Social Security taxable. She found making the higher quarterly estimated tax payments was straining her budget. What she needed was a more tax-efficient way to generate income.

Shirley lived in a single family home where she had raised her children and didn't really want to move. However, she was considering the option of selling her home and moving into a smaller condominium that would hopefully be less costly to maintain.

When Shirley came to me for financial advice, I found she considered herself to be a moderate investor. She knew growth would be needed to help keep pace with inflation. Her accounts were invested equally in stocks and bonds. Like most Americans, she had invested both her taxable account and IRA the same way. Could there have been a better way to allocate the investments from a tax-efficient standpoint and still maintain the moderate risk allocation?

The answer was yes—an answer supported by a study from Robert Dammon and Chester Spatt, finance professors at Carnegie Mellon. Dammon and Spatt published a study in the *Journal of Finance*[1] that showed some simple rules of thumb. Their first assertion was investors should put their taxable fixed-income investments (government bonds, corporate bonds, and certificates of deposit or CDs) along with real estate investment trusts (which are mostly taxed at ordinary income tax rates) into tax-deferred accounts. Ordinary income tax rates can be as high as 39.6%, but long-term capital gains and qualified dividends are taxed at a maximum rate of 15% (20% for taxpayers in the highest bracket), so the stock assets should be placed in taxable accounts. The study found this allocation was beneficial even for those who trade stocks frequently.

> **RICK'S TIP:** Note that calculating taxes can get complicated, because it depends on how long you hold the security and whether the accounts will be subject to state income tax.

Thus, putting the most highly taxed assets into tax-deferred accounts like an IRA or 401(k), and holding those with tax preferred treatment like stocks and stock mutual funds, which generate long-term capital gains and qualified dividends, can easily add 20% in portfolio value over time. This is especially true for middle-aged investors who have a longer period to compound.

Some investors would argue it doesn't matter if you hold bonds in a taxable account, because they'd only invest in tax-free municipal bonds. Dammon and Spatt's study concluded municipal bonds should only be used in taxable accounts after the tax-deferred accounts have been filled with taxable bonds. The reasoning is that municipals historically pay a much lower yield than taxable bonds. Earning the higher returns on the taxable bonds in a tax-deferred account more than offsets the tax paid when you have to start draw-ing from those accounts and paying tax on the distributions.

The disadvantage is compounded if you end up holding stocks in the tax-deferred account because you're holding municipal bonds in the taxable account. You lose the 15% tax treatment on your capi-tal gains and dividends, because all withdrawals from tax-deferred accounts are taxed as ordinary income. The investor could end up paying as much as 39.6% on the capital gains earned from stock holdings in an IRA.

Paying the lower tax rates on stocks is just one advantage of hold-ing them in a taxable account. The other comes from the reality that not every stock investment is going to work out favorably. Every port-folio is going to have some losers from time to time. Taking a loss in a taxable account allows you to write off that loss against other income. Capital losses will offset capital gains one-to-one. In the event you have a net loss, you can write it off against other income up to $3,000 in one tax year. Losses in excess of $3,000 can be car-ried forward to future tax years until they can be used. Losses in a tax-deferred account can't be used on your tax return.

The argument we frequently hear against this strategy surrounds the need for a lump sum withdrawal when the stock market is down. What if you need to take out $50,000 in the middle of a stock mar-ket correction? Wouldn't you be putting yourself in a situation where you bought high and are now selling low? Shouldn't you keep some money in bonds in the taxable account for this situation? Not at all. The objective in this situation isn't to reduce your stock holdings in a down market.

To accomplish this, we'd sell $50,000 of the stock security in the taxable account and simultaneously sell $50,000 of a bond in the tax-deferred account. With the proceeds from the bond sale, we'd buy $50,000 of the same security. You've effectively taken your with-drawal from the bond side of your portfolio.

In Shirley's case, we were able to move all of her bonds to her IRA account and replace the bonds with stock mutual funds in her

RICK'S TIP: Be careful if you're selling a security in your taxable account at a loss. This would trigger a wash sale if you buy the exact same security in your IRA within 30 days before or after the sale, and the loss won't be allowed. In this situation, you want to buy another stock or stock fund but not the exact one you just sold at a loss.

taxable account. Using the asset allocation strategy advocated in the next section, we selected diversified stock mutual funds that complemented her other stock holdings. We also replaced the stock fund holdings she had that were underperforming or not already tax efficient. By holding a small cash position and periodically selling portions of her stock funds to replenish it, she was able to take monthly distributions that equaled the income she'd been receiving.

Finally, we arranged to have her tax liability withheld from her RMD at the end of each year. This eliminated the need to make quarterly estimates. Paying the tax liability at the end of the year also allowed her to retain earnings on the tax payment longer than if she had to send in the money four times per year. Her cash flow improved significantly, and her total tax bill was reduced by 15%.

Begin to Build Your Investment Plan Around Asset Allocation

In 1986, Gary Brinson, Randolph Hood, and Gilbert Beebower analyzed 90 pension funds and identified three primary investment strategies that determine variations in portfolio performance: (1) market timing, (2) security selection, and (3) asset allocation.[2] Out of these three strategies, the two that have the *least* impact on performance variation are market timing and security selection, activities that rely on attempts to predict the future. Most stockbrokers' recommendations are based on these two strategies.

Transfer Highly Taxed Assets Into Tax-Deferred Accounts

- Decide on your allocation between stocks and bonds, then allocate all of your bonds to your tax-deferred accounts first. If you're allocating part of your portfolio to real estate investment trusts, these securities should also be put into the tax-deferred accounts first.
- Only use municipal bonds in your taxable account after you've filled your tax-deferred accounts with bonds.
- When taking a withdrawal from your taxable account in a down market, simultaneously sell the same dollar amount of bonds in the tax-deferred account as you do of stocks in the taxable account. Then use the bond sale proceeds to buy stocks in the tax-deferred account to maintain your overall balance.

Wall Street firms spend billions of dollars each year trying to out-guess their competition in these two areas. Yet on average, the two strategies don't add value. In most studies, not only are they found to not add value, but especially after management fees are deducted, they significantly underperform the market.

The third strategy in the Brinson Hood Beebower study—asset allocation—has the largest effect on portfolio performance variation and is the simplest of the three to use. Nobel Prize–winning economist Harry Markowitz used asset allocation as the basis of his modern portfolio theory (MPT), which has become the standard for the best advisers in the business today. (I'll describe both asset allocation and MPT in more detail in the next section.)

The importance of asset allocation is evidenced in the annual study on Qualitative Analysis of Investor Behavior (QAIB) published by DALBAR, a firm that develops standards for—and provides research, ratings, and rankings of intangible factors to—the financial services industry. In 1994 the QAIB effort began to examine the returns investors actually realize and the behaviors that produce those returns. The 2014 QAIB study found an average retail mutual fund investor grew $10,000 to only $26,634 during the 20-year period ending December 31, 2013, earning 5.02% per year. A buy and hold strategy using the S&P 500 index grew that same $10,000 into $58,350, earning 9.22% per year.

Image 2-1, from the 2014 QAIB study[3], illustrates how mutual fund inflows and outflows compared with the direction of the S&P 500 Index during 2013.

DALBAR observed "Correcting the folly of market timing can be approached in one of two ways. The first is to guess correctly instead of incorrectly. This approach is unrealistic and clearly does nothing to alleviate the market timing problem, in fact only serves to reinforce it. A second way to avoid market timing pitfalls is to not time the market but instead adopt a buy and hold strategy that has rewarded prudent and patient investors for decades."[4]

Whether the mutual fund industry is enjoying rapid expansion in times of economic boom or is being battered by the bears, the key findings uncovered in DALBAR's first study remain true:

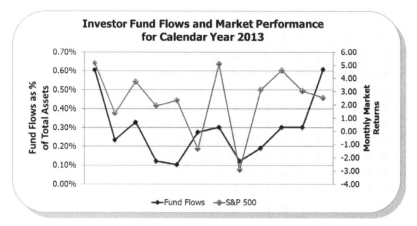

Image 2-1

1. Investment return is far more dependent on investor behavior than on fund performance.
2. Mutual fund investors who hold their investments are more successful than those that time the market.

Asset allocation accounts for more than 90% of the variation in returns of a diversified portfolio! So why isn't everyone using it? Many advisers continue to attempt to add value to your accounts through market-timing, otherwise known as active trading strategies. (I go into more detail about active trading strategies in the next section.) Advisers follow these traditional investment strategies, strategies many academic studies and publications—including this book—conclude don't work. Most stockbrokers and active managers simply don't understand the concepts featured in this book or choose to ignore them. Why?

Wall Street has become the accepted authority and its wisdom goes unchallenged. The people who work on Wall Street have the mistaken impression they're at the center of the financial universe. Huge salaries and extravagant livelihoods are based on the belief that active investment management adds value and is worth the cost. If Wall Street were to follow the concepts of investing by utilizing asset classes, it would literally be out of business. Of course, nobody's going to rush to put the Street out of business, so an active strategy continues to be utilized. Yet, active strategies engender investigation and analysis expenses, and increase general transaction costs, including capital gains taxation. They also often require the acceptance of a relatively high degree of diversifiable risk.

Despite the overwhelming power of Wall Street, even the most senior members of the investment community have fortunately begun to question why asset allocation hasn't had more widespread acceptance.[5] It turns out the organizational politics of the major financial services firms have proven to be another formidable barrier to its acceptance.

Yet another barrier to asset allocation acceptance is the irrational behaviors many individual investors display. These behaviors make investors more likely to accept the advice of ill-informed financial planners. Be on the lookout for the following six irrational behaviors in yourself:

1. **Loss aversion.** If you expect to always find high returns with low risk, you're fooling yourself. Consider what happened in the summer of 1982, when large American banks lost close to all of their past earnings (cumulatively)—amounting to just about everything ever made in the history of American banking. These banks had been lending to South and Central American countries that all defaulted at the same time—"an event of an exceptional nature."[6] It took just one summer to figure out this was a sucker's business, and all of the earnings from these ventures came from a very risky game. The bankers involved had led everyone, especially themselves, into believing they weren't taking high risks. They thought they were being conservative. In truth, they weren't conservative, just phenomenally skilled at self-deception. This travesty is repeating itself once again today, with the "risk-conscious" large banks again under financial strain after the real-estate subprime loan collapse.

2. **Narrow framing or tunneling.** This includes making decisions without considering all implications. Avoid tunneling at all costs, because it can take you off in a wrong direction. We're taught that intense focus like this is a principle for success, but focus too narrowly, and you miss the bigger picture.

3. **Anchoring.** This term means to relate to familiar experiences even when inappropriate, or to take undue risk in one area and avoid rational risk in others.

4. **Ineffective diversification.** This is diversification in its worst sense: seeking to reduce risk, but by simply using different sources. It involves herding or copying

the behavior of others, even in the face of unfavorable outcomes.

5. **Regret.** With regret, you treat errors of commission more seriously than errors of omission. You may have a tendency to react to news without reasonable examination.

6. **Optimism.** In optimism, you believe only good things happen to you, and bad things are meant for others.

5 Steps to Reducing the Wrong Kind of Investment Risk

A good way to avoid the irrational behaviors I described in the last section is to take the following five steps toward reducing your overall investment risk. Knowing and practicing these steps before potential problems arise can increase your odds of steering clear of actions that will hurt your retirement assets. Perhaps no one understands this better than Harry Markowitz.

Build Your Investment Plan Around Asset Allocation

- Asset allocation is far more important than both market timing and security selection in making sure your portfolio performs well.
- Be aware many advisers ignore asset allocation and instead engage in market timing—or active trading strategies, because a flurry of activity makes it appear they're adding value to your account.
- Irrational behaviors on the part of investors themselves contribute to a reluctance to embrace asset allocation in favor of other ineffective strategies.

Sixty years ago, Markowitz, a graduate student at the University of Chicago, developed the principle of modern portfolio theory (MPT) based on his keen insight: Risk (which he defined as volatility) must be the central focus for the whole process of investing. Markowitz observed an investment world blindly living in a paradox—while it was accepted that human beings, by nature, are risk-averse, investing had essentially ignored the inter-relationship between risk and return. That is, to achieve returns, *risk is necessary.* But how can you control it?

MPT answers this question through its postulation the total risk in a portfolio can be separated into two kinds of risk: uncompensated risk and compensated risk. Uncompensated risk (about 70% of total risk) is the possibility economic (and non-economic) news may uniquely impact the market price of a *particular* stock. For example, the price of Ford Motor Co. stock may go down as a result of the departure of a key Ford executive. Investors can protect themselves against this risk by also owning stock in companies that are unaffected by the departure of Ford executives.

Compensated risk (about 30% of total risk) reflects the economic (and non-economic) news that impacts the market price of *many or all* stocks. Because the prices of individual stocks are affected, more or less, by the risk of a general rise or fall in the value of the stock market itself, compensated risk is unavoidable by an investor who invests in the stock market. When investors bear compensated risk, however, they expect to be rewarded for doing so.

Markowitz was subsequently awarded the Nobel Prize for Economic Sciences in 1990. Merton H. Miller, who shared the prize, called their theory the "Big Bang of modern finance." Indeed, investment managers began to apply techniques of the theory in the late 1960s, and by the 1970s, they'd become commonplace. Now taught in virtually every graduate business school in the country, modern portfolio theory stipulates if you're going to take the risks of the stock market, you need to be compensated for those risks.

In terms of your own retirement assets, the question you should be asking is: *How can I protect my portfolio from uncompensated risk while in pursuit of higher returns?* Most advisers have no idea they can eliminate virtually all uncompensated risk and reduce overall volatility by following an investment process that utilizes the following five steps:

1. Asset Class Investing

An asset class is simply a group of securities that share common risk and return characteristics. Asset class investing involves the construction of portfolios that reliably deliver the returns of a specific asset class. This is done by investing in all, or most, of the securities within the asset category under consideration. There's no subjective forecasting of the stock market or economic conditions and no attempt to distinguish between "undervalued" and "overvalued" securities. Securities are considered for purchase when they meet the asset class parameters defined by the investment manager, and they're considered for sale when they don't.

The three main asset classes include: **cash/money markets, bonds,** and **stocks.** While these asset classes appear in an order that's generally the safest to the most risky, remember there's no absolute ranking of risk in the equity market. Let's take a closer look at each of the classes now.

CASH/MONEY MARKET

The first asset class, cash, includes money market funds, which are made up of T-Bills, certificates of deposit (CDs), and commercial paper. These investments are called cash because money market funds seek to maintain a stable value of $1 per share; in other words, the price should not fluctuate. Few people understand when their holdings are in cash, they're also invested in an asset class: the U.S. dollar.

BONDS

Also called fixed-income, this asset class is divided into two main groups: stable bonds such as U.S. government and AAA corporate bonds, certificates of deposits (CDs), and tax-free municipal bonds; and higher-yield bonds such as BB corporate bonds and junk bonds. For my clients, I generally recommend only the first group. Within this category, my clients and I decide if we want long-term, intermediate, or shorter-duration bonds. I recommend short-term bonds, meaning five to seven years or less to maturity, because a short-duration fund will give you 94% of the return without the long-term bond volatility. If you're in a long-term bond fund and interest rates move up, your fund can drop 25% in a day.

I also prefer my clients own the individual bonds themselves rather than through a fund. Owning the individual bond gives you a fixed interest rate and a fixed date in the future when you can expect you'll get your principal returned in full.

STOCKS

After cash and bonds, we subdivide asset classes into more specific categories distinguished by their unique characteristics. Equity, or stock, asset classes are often categorized according to the size of their market capitalization (number of outstanding shares multiplied by current stock price). What stocks go into an asset class? The way the

RICK'S TIP: Beware of chasing yield in fixed-income investments. Investments don't pay 6% in a 2% environment unless risk is involved. If you don't understand the risk or don't think any risk exists, you should run the other way. Raymond DeVoe, Jr. wisely pointed out in 1995, "More money has been lost reaching for yield than at the point of a gun."[7]

academics built equity asset classes is quite involved. First, they took all of the companies on the New York Stock Exchange, ranked them by size, and then divided them into 10 deciles. They designated the largest one tenth of the companies as Decile Number 1. This group included companies on the scale of General Electric or Apple Inc. Decile Number 2 represented the next 10% graduating down in company size. Deciles 9 and 10 were the smallest companies, the bottom 20% in size.

Next, they looked at the NASDAQ and the American stock exchange, and they filled in the same capitalization requirements that were in Deciles 1 through 10. Deciles 1 through 5 qualify as large company stocks; small company stocks are in the 6 through 10 deciles. Deciles 9 and 10 on the NASDAQ and American stock exchange have more than 2,000 small stocks. The academic asset class of value stocks originally included every value stock, across all those same markets. They discovered that was too cumbersome, so they divided it into asset classes called "large value" and "small value." The same applies to "growth" and "international" equity asset classes. Asset classes for stocks are further refined in this way according to their potential total return over time. Check out some of the primary asset classes:

- **Large-Cap Growth.** These are very large companies with an average capitalization of approximately $10 billion or greater. This type of company shows strong growth rates both historic and projected forward. These companies historically have a growth rate for the past five years of 5–7% with similar projections for the next five years.
- **U.S. Large-Cap Value.** These are large U.S. publicly traded companies (average capitalization of approximately $10 billion or greater) that may be temporarily out of favor. They aren't doing well as measured by their price to earnings ratio and/or are distressed economically based on book value.

- **U.S. Mid-Cap Growth.** These are U.S. publicly traded medium-sized companies with an average capitalization between $2 billion and $10 billion. They have good sales and good prospects for the future. These companies historically have a growth rate for the past five years of 7–10% with similar projections for the next five years.
- **U.S. Mid-Cap Value.** These are U.S. publicly traded medium-sized companies with an average capitalization between $2 billion and $10 billion that are out of favor.
- **U.S. Small-Cap Growth.** These are U.S. publicly traded smaller companies with an average capitalization between $300 million and $2 billion. They have good sales and good prospects for the future. These companies historically have a growth rate for the past five years of 10%+ with similar projections for the next five years.
- **U.S. Small-Cap Value.** These are U.S. publicly traded smaller companies (with an average capitalization between $300 million and $2 billion) that are out of favor.
- **International (Developed).** This group generally comprises stocks of companies based outside the United States—from any part of the world with a developed economy. These stocks are based in countries with a relatively high level of economic growth and security. A developed country will tend to have a high gross domestic product per capita income, a good general standard of living, and a well-established level of industrialization with a built-out infrastructure (e.g., transportation, communications).
- **International (Emerging Markets).** This group generally comprises stocks of companies based outside the United States—from any part of the world with an economy progressing toward becoming advanced. Emerging markets generally do not have the level of market

efficiency and strict standards in accounting and securities regulation as developed countries. They do typically have a physical financial infrastructure including banks, a stock exchange, and a unified currency.

Asset class funds are called passively managed, which means there's no "active" decision-making occurring about buying and selling the issues that are contained within the mutual fund. Their sole purpose is to mimic the markets while experiencing very low turnover.

On the flip side, actively managed mutual funds (especially the advertised ones that appeal to the retail market) tend to do what we call *style drift*. Active managers are under tremendous pressure to deliver returns, even though that may not be the function of a particular fund. They'll drift out of their asset class into another asset class in an effort to hopefully boost their returns.

It's more difficult to maintain a balanced portfolio with actively managed funds because of style drift. Let's say you wanted a portfolio that's a 50-50 mix of large-growth companies and small-value companies. If the manager of the fund of large-growth companies starts buying small-value companies because large growth isn't doing well, or vice versa, that skews your 50-50 allocation.

In addition, if every fund went to large growth when growth is doing well, then growth plummets, your whole portfolio would plummet. That's why many investors lost 40–70% when the technology bubble burst in the 2000–2002 market. They may have tried to remain diversified, but the managers of those funds drifted. If each one fudged just a little in the direction of whatever was up at the time, it would be enough to cause big trouble in a portfolio.

Another example is how most 401(k) plans are marketed. Normally, the provider offers a list of mutual funds from which participants may choose. This places all the responsibility on the employee. Participants, without any knowledge or advice, naturally pick the funds with the best returns for the last period, and often end up with everything in one asset class.

I feel the best way to do asset class investing is by owning asset class mutual funds and ETFs or institutional asset class mutual funds, because they're more reliable in concentrating on a specific asset class. These funds are a relatively new hybrid, created by institutional money managers. Although not available to the general public, institutional asset class mutual funds can be purchased by participants through selected groups of investment advisers who are required to educate their clients on the benefits of passive asset class investing.

There are three major attributes of institutional asset class funds that attract institutional investors:

1. **Lower operating expenses.** All mutual funds and separately managed accounts have expenses that include management fees, administrative charges, and custody fees. These are expressed as a percentage of assets. The average annual expense ratio for equity mutual funds was 0.77% in 2012.[8] In comparison, the same ratio for institutional asset class funds is typically only about one-half of all retail equity mutual funds. All other factors being equal, lower costs lead to higher rates of return.

2. **Lower turnover resulting in lower cost.** Most investment managers do a lot of active trading thinking this adds value. According to The Motley Fool Website, actively managed funds have an average turnover ratio of 85%.[9] This means, on average, 85% of the securities in the portfolio are traded over a 12-month period. This represents $85,000 of traded securities for every $100,000 invested. Higher turnover is costly to shareholders, because each time a trade is made, there are transaction costs, including commissions, spreads, and market impact costs. These hidden costs may amount to more than a fund's total operating expenses if the fund trades heavily, or if it invests in small company stocks for which trading costs

are very high. Institutional asset class funds have significantly lower turnover, because their institutional investors want them to deliver a specific asset class return with as low a cost as possible.

3. **Lower turnover resulting in lower taxes.** If a mutual fund sells a security for a gain, it must make a capital gains distribution to shareholders. Mutual funds are required to distribute most of their taxable income each year, including realized gains, to stay tax-exempt at the corporate level. Therefore, they distribute all of their income annually, as no mutual fund manager wants to have his or her performance reduced by paying corporate income taxes.

2. Asset Allocation

Asset allocation simply means determining what proportion of your money is going to be invested in which asset classes (stocks, bonds, and cash investments) in order to maximize the growth of your portfolio for each unit of risk you take. As I mentioned earlier, this may

RICK'S TIP: The Brinson et al. study I referenced earlier also revealed when two portfolios have the same arithmetic average return, the portfolio with smaller up and down swings in value (less volatility) will have a greater compound return. Moreover, it showed 94% of performance was attributable to the allocation of the assets. The study's authors found even choosing the right individual asset added less than 6% to the returns. The factor that made the greatest difference was the combination or allocation of asset classes.[10]

be the single most important determinant of the long-term performance of any investment portfolio.

Some critics of asset allocation see this balance as settling for mediocrity, but for most investors, it's the best protection against major loss should things ever go amiss in one investment class or sub-class. The consensus among most informed financial professionals is asset allocation is one of the most important decisions investors make.

Allocating your assets is simple. The first step is to identify what asset classes are represented by the mutual funds. Then you can spread, or allocate, your money among them to minimize risk. How do you determine what percentage of each asset class you should own? For every level of risk, there's some optimum combination of investments that will give you the highest rate of return. The combinations of investments exhibiting this optimal risk/reward trade-off form what we call the efficient frontier, as indicated in Image 2-2.

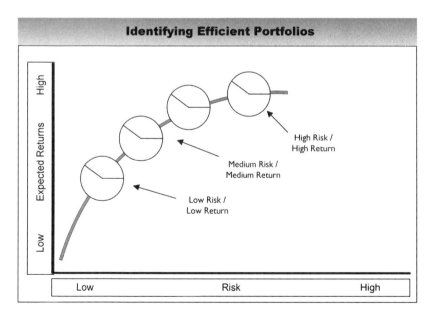

Image 2-2

You can choose how much volatility you're willing to bear in your portfolio by picking any point that falls on the efficient frontier. This will give you the maximum return for the amount of risk you wish to accept. Optimizing your portfolio isn't something you can calculate in your head. There are computer programs that are dedicated to determining optimal portfolios by estimating hundreds (and sometimes thousands) of different expected returns for each given amount of risk. Your financial adviser should be able to offer you an effective program for determining your own optimal portfolio.

3. Diversification

The most common definition of diversification is not putting all of your eggs (i.e., your investments) in one basket. A truly diversified portfolio is comprised of many asset classes, some of which are doing well, and some of which aren't.

Some investors believe they've effectively diversified simply by holding a number of different stocks. They don't realize they're in for an emotional roller-coaster ride if these investments share similar risk factors by belonging to the same industry group or asset class. For instance, "diversification" among many high-tech companies isn't diversification at all.

I've found most investors are surprised to learn asset classes switch places, variably outperforming each other. In general, I see most people load up on blue chip stocks, which fall under the large

RICK'S TIP: Although concentrated ownership of founders' stock sometimes conveys fabulous riches to a fortunate few (e.g., Microsoft's Bill Gates), it's impossible to know ahead of time which firms will grow from unseasoned startups to Fortune 500 companies. In fact, it's reasonable to expect a great percentage of new companies will fail.

cap growth asset class I mentioned earlier (which, by the way, is the most common type of asset sold to them by their stockbrokers). Why is this? Because large-cap stocks are the names that are the most recognizable, like IBM, Wal-Mart, Microsoft, and General Electric.

If all of your money is in several investments, yet in only one asset class, then your investment portfolio is ineffectively diversified, meaning all of your funds move together, and you really only have one asset class investment. Only when each of your investments move independently in the market can your portfolio be effectively diversified; see Step 4 below for a more detailed discussion on this. A diversified portfolio provides stability and, hence, a larger long-term return, but only if you spread your money among the various asset classes that don't always have the same price movements—for example, between value and growth; small and large; or international growth and value. Therefore, the total return of a diversified portfolio will never be as good as the current best asset class, nor will it ever be as poor as the worst. But the overall ride will be smoother, and the end result could be a superior return.

4. Effective Diversification

Almost all diversification is good, but the academics have refined it down to what they call effective and ineffective diversification. Again, an example of ineffective diversification is the investor who holds Microsoft stock and decides to diversify by investing in Dell and six other similar computer companies. If anything affects the computer industry, all the investments will be *positively correlated* to move together, either up or down.

Effective diversification means selecting asset classes with a low correlation to each other—an approach Harry Markowitz acknowledged when he stated that though almost all diversification is good, there's effective diversification and ineffective diversification.

Image 2-3 shows the increases and decreases of value for two portfolios over time. The top chart shows ineffective diversification,

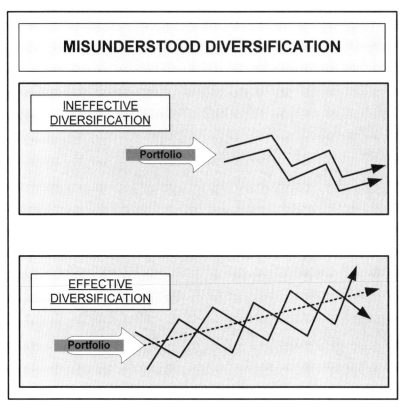

Image 2-3

in which the portfolios change in tandem with each other, and the second chart demonstrates effective diversification, in which the two portfolios move opposite to each other.

Overall, the charts indicate two equal investments can have the same arithmetic rate of return but have very different ending values because of volatility. If your investments move up and down together, they are ineffectively diversified, having the same effect as if they were all invested in just one fund. Chances are, there's tremendous stock overlap in these two ineffectively diversified funds as well.

Selecting asset classes with a low correlation to each other (i.e., effective diversification) is the Nobel Prize–winning secret for achieving more consistent portfolio performance. Again, academics have actually calculated methods to measure correlation in a portfolio, thereby enabling the volatility or risk of a portfolio to be measured with greater degrees of predictability. You want to design your portfolio to have as little volatility as necessary to achieve your goals.

5. Rebalancing

Most investors and their advisers hold fast to the belief they should keep their winners and sell their losers. This leads to portfolios with a large majority of current winners that become losers when the market turns, which it always has.

Rebalancing is a disciplined process of selling the winning asset classes and repositioning the proceeds into the so-called "losing" asset classes—an automatic version of selling high and buying low, which is how you ultimately win at investing.

The principle of rebalancing is to maintain the same percentages in the various asset classes you've chosen, to maintain proper diversification in all market environments. By rebalancing, you may give up some short-term gains if you reduce your holdings of winning stocks prematurely, but you'll also miss the big losses if and when they collapse.

The way to rebalance your original portfolio is to review it regularly with your adviser. You want to rebalance when the stock markets are reaching new highs, so you can harvest the gains in your stocks. This is the time to move some of those gains to the bond side of your portfolio, so you don't give all of your gains back the next time the stock market sells off. You also want to do this in the most tax-effective manner through harvesting losses in the taxable accounts and placing the bonds in your tax-deferred accounts.

Before the tech bubble burst, many smart investment advisers rebalanced their equity positions down to their allocation targets as the bull market pushed equity values upward. They increased equity positions as the declining markets dropped those positions below targets. As a result, they were selling high, then buying low. See the

RICK'S TIP: Studies show more frequent rebalancing improves results, which would indicate a style that's outperforming the broad market doesn't stay in favor for long periods of time. The same holds true for a style that's underperforming the broad market: Its out-of-favor status doesn't remain for long periods of time.

logic? When the price is down, you're able to buy more shares. Plus, you're reinvesting the money you've made along with your principal and compounding your growth.

Rebalancing an investment portfolio seems simple on the surface, but as you start to think through the method, frequency, tolerance limits, fees, and commissions, the subject reveals itself to be quite complex and without easy answers. Your adviser should be knowledgeable about the various issues surrounding rebalancing and, ideally, should be able to explain them to you in a way that makes the desired method acceptable and practical to apply.

How to Invest in a Tax-Efficient Way

Now let's discuss how to ensure your investment portfolio is efficient, not just from a risk perspective, but from a tax standpoint as well. You may not be able to control the market, but you do have a lot of control over your taxes. By understanding basic tax rules and using tax-efficient investment strategies, you can minimize the annual tax bite on your taxable accounts.

The most tax-efficient investment strategy is simple: Hold shares for as long as possible, thus deferring the taxes on your capital gains until you sell. An extremely tax-efficient portfolio would therefore be a selection of growth stocks you bought and held for the long haul. In this case, growth stocks would be preferred, because they tend to pay little or no dividends. Your return would be mostly made up of

Reduce Investment Risk

The five steps work together to help level out the up-and-down ride associated with good and bad markets, producing steadier overall results:

1. Asset class investing
2. Asset allocation
3. Diversification
4. Effective diversification
5. Rebalancing

These powerful investment strategies work equally well for conservative, moderate, or aggressive investors. You can use them to build your own portfolio for retirement, to protect your assets once you've retired, or to meet other financial goals. Amazingly, the strategies actually simplify the investment decision-making process.

long-term capital gains. Best of all, you'd get to decide when to pay the tax by choosing when to sell them.

However, a portfolio full of growth stocks isn't without problems. For starters, concentration in few securities and the lack of diversification from being in mostly one asset class create volatility. You need the diversification of a balanced portfolio over several asset classes to reduce this volatility. It's important to keep in mind, then, that investing tax efficiently is a balancing act. Though the reality is there will always be trade-offs, your overarching goal should be to minimize taxes while still attempting to achieve superior investment returns.

Another issue with long-term investments is they tend to scare some investors into holding even when it's not wise to do so, because these investors believe selling would trigger additional capital gains. Remember: *The tax decision should never overrule the investment decision.* Assessing the tax consequences of your investments at each stage—contribution, accumulation, and distribution—is the key to success in the world of tax-advantaged investing. Just don't lose sight of the investment return like one of my clients, Joe Mitchell, unfortunately did.

CASE STUDY

Joe Mitchell, investor

Joe Mitchell had accumulated a large position in a well-known computer company stock. He purchased most of the stock in the 1990s, and through several stock splits, he'd accumulated more than $250,000 worth of the stock with a total cost of $50,000.

The stock had been doing well until 2005, when the stock price started heading south. By the middle of the year, Joe's stock was down more than 10%, yet the stock market was still going up. Still, Joe refused to sell any of the stock, because he didn't want to pay capital gains tax. By the end of the year, his stock value had fallen to less than $178,000, and the stock market was up that year by 4.9%.

Had Joe sold the stock when it was down 10%, he would've owed $26,000 in capital gains tax ($225,000 − $50,000 = $175,000 × 15%). He would've been left with $199,000 that could have gained back 4.9% in an index fund.

Joe's mistake is easy to see in hindsight (the perfect vision!). Of course, you won't know at the time if the stock's going to recover or if the investment you choose with the proceeds is going to perform better than the one you just sold. But in Joe's case, the stock was moving at such a sharp contrast to the stock market's overall direction he should've at least sold part of the position by mid-year. His stock position went on to lose 16% in 2006 (S&P 500 +15.8%) and another 2% in 2007 (S&P 500 +5.5%). Again, investment reasons should always trump tax implications.

RICK'S TIP: If mutual funds are the building blocks of a portfolio, tax-efficient investing begins with the simple notion that good fund managers who are sensitive to tax issues can make a difference on your after-tax return. A "good manager" from a tax perspective harvests losses, pays attention to the holding period, and controls the fund's turnover rate. Studies show the average actively managed mutual fund operates at 85% tax efficiency.

Most fund managers are tasked solely with generating a return. They don't think about working with taxable and non-taxable portfolios, and they don't care about short-term gains. Of course, in your IRA or 401(k), you don't care about short-term gains either, but short-term gains in a taxable account can be disastrous. However, mutual fund managers are often not as concerned as you are with keeping taxes low. These professionals are concentrating on maximizing pre-tax, not after-tax, returns. The difference is an important one.

It's clear the best after-tax returns start with the best pre-tax returns, but even the fund industry itself has come around to the need for examining after-tax returns. Let's dig in with an explanation of the more tax-efficient types of funds.

- **Passive mutual funds.** Passive mutual funds are usually designed to match the performance and risk character-istics of a market benchmark like the Standard & Poor's (S&P) 500 Index. They've long been the easiest way to construct a tax-smart portfolio. Index funds don't need to do much buying and selling, because the makeup of the portfolio changes only when the underlying bench-mark changes. Because the portfolio turnover in these funds is low, stock index funds can often reduce an investor's tax exposure. But investors should understand there are few absolutes: Index funds can also realize gains. When a security is removed from a fund's target index, stock in the company must be sold by the fund and new stock purchased. Index funds also tend to have lower expense ratios because they aren't actively managed. Lower expenses mean you get to keep more of the gain in your pocket.

- **Exchange-traded funds (ETFs).** Exchange-traded funds (ETFs) are a popular alternative to mutual funds due to their tax efficiency and lower operating fees. The fact ETFs offer more control over management of gains is very attractive to the tax-efficient investor. ETFs look like index funds but trade like stocks. The most popular ETFs use broad market benchmarks such as the S&P 500 Index or the Nasdaq 100 (QQQs or Qubes). There are ETFs that represent nearly all parts of the market (mid-sized value, small growth, and foreign companies) as well as various sectors (telecom, utilities, technology). Most ETFs have even lower expenses than their index fund counterparts. Unlike mutual funds, ETFs can be bought and sold throughout the day, rather than just at the end of trading. ETFs tend to have little turnover, few capital gains distributions, and a low dividend yield— making them very tax efficient.

In addition, ETFs aren't vulnerable to the hysteria of other investors because liquidity is provided through the stock market. When the stock market declines, many investors panic and pull out. Mutual fund managers are then forced to sell positions to provide cash to the sellers. Those shareholders that keep their shares suffer a double whammy: a loss of market value and taxable gains created by the manager selling securities in the fund. Many investors have no idea this can happen. ETFs do not need to sell securities to meet redemptions. Despite their benefits, ETFs pose a problem for individual investors in that there is typically a modest transaction fee to buy and sell them. If you're investing regular sums over time, those costs can easily negate any break you get on annual expenses.

- **Tax-efficient mutual funds.** Some types of mutual funds are more tax-friendly than others. Tax-efficient mutual funds, for example, are managed by professional fund managers who attempt to minimize the buying and selling of securities and thus are less likely to pass along taxable gains to individual investors. These professionals use a variety of strategies and objectives, including indexing and careful security selection, to offset most capital gains with capital losses.

  These funds are actively managed, but by managers who pay attention to the tax ramifications of their trading. Some simply keep turnover low, minimizing the capital gains they have to realize. Others try to match the sale of any winners with dumping their losers, so gains can be offset by losses.

Review Your Portfolio

Tax-efficient investing requires active involvement. That starts with looking for tax-efficient mutual funds as discussed above. You also need to monitor the portfolios so losses are harvested to offset gains. In addition, you must pay attention to holding periods to ensure the asset has been held at least 12 months.

Start by screening your funds for performance and then for tax efficiency. Separate your list of funds that meet your performance criteria by tax efficiency. You don't want to completely exclude funds that aren't tax efficient, because these can be held in your tax-deferred

RICK'S TIP: You can still rebalance in a taxable account. As long as you've held the stocks or stock funds at least a year, you'll benefit from a lower capital gains rate. This allows you to improve your investment portfolio without major suffering at tax time. Many investors unknowingly expose themselves to unnecessarily high rates of income taxes when they sell shares from their taxable investment account at a profit prior to holding the position for 12 months. One strategy for rebalancing in taxable accounts is to take all distributions in cash instead of reinvesting the distributions back into the original fund. The cash can be used to invest in the underweighted parts of the portfolio. This can avoid the need to sell positions to rebalance.

accounts. You don't need or want to be in a tax-efficient fund with your qualified retirement plan. Remember the trade-offs I mentioned earlier between performance and tax efficiency? Returns tend to be lower in tax-efficient funds. Inside a qualified plan, you want the managers to be more aggressive and make moves in the portfolio. If they considered the tax consequences, they might choose not to make those moves.

One of the biggest mistakes investors make is failing to harvest losses in their portfolio. Many people think just because an investment is worth less than they paid for it, they haven't really lost any money, because they didn't sell it. Tell that to the holders of Enron stock! You should start by evaluating the investment. If you had cash today, would you still invest in that same position, or are there other opportunities that look better? If you would not invest today, take the loss and reinvest elsewhere. The loss could be worth thousands in saved taxes. The reason most investors don't use this strategy is because loss harvesting is labor intensive—and nobody wants to admit to taking a loss.

Tax-Efficient Investing

- Investing tax efficiently is a balancing act between diversified asset classes that minimize taxes yet still achieve superior returns.
- The tax decision should never overrule the investment decision.
- Index funds, exchange-traded funds, and tax-efficient mutual funds are all good tax-efficient investment choices.
- In terms of your retirement accounts, tax efficiency shouldn't be your goal; your retirement account investments should be more aggressive so they result in bigger returns over the long haul.
- Review your portfolio regularly, and don't be afraid to harvest losses—especially because you may be able to take the losses as a tax write-off.

Implement a Zero Tax Bracket Approach

Recent tax legislation has made it much easier to construct a tax-efficient portfolio. The initial act came in 2003 with the Jobs and Growth Tax Relief Reconciliation Act (JGTRRA) of 2003, which was then extended by the Tax Increase Prevention and Reconciliation Act (TIPRA) of 2005. These tax cuts drove the top federal capital-gains rate down to 15% and made the same rate apply to dividends issued by domestic stocks and mutual funds. These laws became permanent with the passage of the American Taxpayer Relief Act of 2012. If your taxable income puts you in the 10–15% bracket (that's $75,300 or less for married filing jointly in 2016, half that for singles), your capital gains and dividends rate is zero. (Keep in mind payouts from foreign stocks and real estate investment trusts don't qualify for the dividend tax break; for maximum tax efficiency, these investments should be held in tax-advantaged retirement accounts.) You can read about these breaks in the following case study about my clients Bob and Carolyn Whitehall.

CASE STUDY

Bob and Carolyn Whitehall, retirees

When Bob Whitehall retired from a regional bank in 1997, he'd accumulated a comfortable nest egg of $1.8 million dollars. A third of his savings was in the common stock of his employer; the bank offered an employee stock purchase program that allowed him to invest in the stock through payroll deduction. The stock had done well over the years, paying cash and stock dividends Bob reinvested while he was working. After retirement, Bob began to take the dividends in cash and used them to supplement his income.

In early 2008, Bob and Carolyn reached their mid-70s, and they came to me for an evaluation of their investment portfolio. I found it was still worth $1.8 million. One third of it was invested in three rental properties; another third was still in the bank's 401(k) plan Bob never rolled over; and the remaining third was invested in various stocks, mutual funds, and bank certificates of deposit (CDs). Bob also still had $500,000 invested in the bank stock that was divided among the 401(k) and the taxable accounts.

Despite only taking modest distributions over the years, the portfolio hadn't appreciated at all. The bank stock had done poorly since his retirement but Bob refused to sell it because he hated paying capital gains tax. The stock had a very low cost basis because he'd accumulated it over many years, and stock dividends aren't taxable until the shares are sold. Still, Bob thought he was being savvy by keeping the stock and not paying capital gains tax.

In reality, the purchasing power of his nest egg had shrunk to $1.3 million because of inflation. Allowing this to continue would eventually reduce Bob and Carolyn's standard of living. If one or both of them ended up in a nursing home, they could see the entire nest egg wiped out in 10 years.

Fortunately, there was an answer that helped even someone like Bob who hated to pay capital gains tax. Today, ordinary income tax rates for individuals range from 10% to 39.6%. Long-term capital gains and qualified dividends (i.e., adjusted net capital gains) are taxed at 15% for taxpayers in the 25–35% bracket, 0% for taxpayers in the 15% or 10% tax brackets, and 20% in the top tax bracket.

In 2016, the 0% rate applies to taxable income up to $37,650 for single taxpayers. The threshold is $75,300 for married couples filing jointly. This number refers to the net taxable income after itemized deductions, as opposed to adjusted gross income (AGI). Thus, a joint filer with an AGI of $100,000 may still be able to take advantage of the 0% bracket if they have itemized deductions of $25,100. That level of deductions isn't difficult to get to if you live in a state that has a high income tax, hold a mortgage on your home, or are charitably minded.

Additionally, you can exceed the taxable income and still receive a partial benefit from the 0% bracket because the portion of your capital gain that's below the threshold would still qualify for the 0% rate. For example, a joint filer with $40,000 in long-term capital gains and $40,000 in other income after deductions would have $34,900 of the gain taxed at 0% and $5,100 taxed at 15%.

My strategy for Bob and Carolyn was to reposition the portfolio to place most of their income-producing assets into their tax-deferred accounts. This significantly reduced their taxable ordinary income, which allowed us to sell more of the stock at the 0% capital gains rate. We sold the bank stock in the 401(k) that had no tax implications and used the proceeds to buy CDs and other fixed-income assets, so they could maintain a balanced investment strategy when investing in tax-efficient investments in the taxable accounts.

Bob wanted to keep some of the bank stock for sentimental reasons, so we agreed to keep $100,000 in the stock. The balance of the stock in their taxable account was sold over the next four years. Bob didn't have to pay capital gains tax on any of the sales proceeds. More importantly, he learned to appreciate the wisdom of evaluating performance on an after-tax basis! It'll be harder for taxpayers who are still working to take advantage of the 0% tax bracket because of the limitations in manipulating earned income.

Retirees who are living on investment income have the most opportunities. Yet one of the challenges for retirees drawing Social Security benefits is structuring income that doesn't make their benefits taxable. This is one of the problems with tax-free municipal bond income: Income from municipal bonds is used in the calculation to determine the taxability of Social Security benefits. When calculating the 0% rate on capital gains, municipal income doesn't count.

Realizing an additional $10,000 in capital gains could make $5,000 more of Social Security subject to tax and potentially put the taxpayer over the 0% bracket. Retirees who are already in a low tax bracket should consider investing in dividend-paying stocks, because they can provide much needed inflation fighting growth potential as well as untaxed income.

You can make the most of the 0% bracket by searching for positions that have the least amount of capital gains. This will allow you to raise the highest amount of tax-free cash. It's an especially desirable method for those retirees who have a significant amount of their assets tied up in tax-deferred accounts.

RICK'S TIP: Retirees drawing Social Security benefits should take care in determining the amount of capital gains they can realize and stay in the 0% bracket. You can review the upcoming section on "Understanding Social Security" to familiarize yourself with the calculation used to tax benefits. Capital gains is income that's used to determine how much of your Social Security is taxed.

Gifting Appreciated Securities

Higher tax bracket investors may want to consider gifting appreciated securities to other family members in the lower tax bracket. If you're considering this strategy, keep in mind the maximum amount you can gift to any one individual without filing a gift tax return is $14,000 in 2016. A husband and wife could gift a total of $28,000 to each child. This amount is adjusted for inflation each year, but only in $1,000 increments.

New kiddie-tax rules also went into effect in 2008. Full-time students younger than 24 are subject to tax at the parents' rates with few exceptions. One of those exceptions is if the child earns income and contributes more than 50% of the cost of his or her support. In this situation, a parent should gift appreciated securities to the student to be sold to pay for college rather than help the student pay for tuition out of pocket. The parent would then be paying for tuition with tax-free dollars using the student's 0% bracket on the capital gain.

Parents who have been helping their adult children fund Roth IRAs should also consider gifting appreciated securities to the child if the child is in the lower tax brackets. The child could then sell the gifted securities to fund the Roth IRA. The ultimate cost to the parent of funding the Roth IRA is less, because the parent is taking advantage of the child's 0% rate on the capital gain.

This same strategy applies to higher income taxpayers who are helping to support their elderly parents that have low taxable income. The taxpayers can transfer appreciated securities to Mom and Dad, who can, in turn, sell the securities to pay for living expenses.

Higher income individuals may want to consider gifting securities with the most amount of appreciation to charities to lower their taxable income. If you aren't comfortable with giving the securities outright to a charity, consider setting up a charitable remainder unitrust (CRUT). Gifting securities to a CRUT is a completed gift and will qualify for a partial tax deduction. A CRUT allows the donor to receive an income stream for life from the gift. The asset is released from the CRUT when the donor passes away. The amount

RICK'S TIP: Part of year-end tax planning should include taking advantage of the 0% tax on long-term capital gains for anyone in the 15% tax bracket. Search your portfolio for long-term gains you can harvest without increasing your income taxes. We don't know how long the 0% tax rate will be remain. Congress is always looking for money, and there's a chance capital gains tax rates could go much higher!

of the deduction is based on the size of the income stream retained by the donor and the donor's life expectancy. Income received from the CRUT is only partially taxable, because part of it is considered a return of capital.

A Zero Tax Bracket Approach

- Taxpayers in the lower income brackets should plan now to take advantage of the 0% rate on long-term capital gains and qualified dividends.
- Higher income taxpayers should look for gifting opportunities to pass appreciated assets to other family members in the lower tax bracket or charities.
- Beware of the tax on Social Security benefits when planning your capital gains strategy. More of your benefits may become taxable and negate a portion of the 0% rate.

You now have two of the three legs of the stool under your belt (great work), but in order to make the stool truly sturdy, you need to know about the all-important Leg Three—tax-free savings—which I cover in-depth in Chapter 3.

Leg Three: Tax-Free Savings Strategies

Understanding Roth Accounts

Tax-free savings strategies is the final leg of my New Three-Legged Stool approach. The main components of this leg are Roth IRAs, Roth 401(k)s, and the new *my* RA. Young or old, you should be constantly looking for ways to use the Roth to control your tax burden both now and in the future. These accounts are the premier individual retirement planning tools and savings accounts offered today, for several reasons I discuss in this chapter.

Roth IRAs

Unlike with traditional IRAs or 401(k)s, withdrawals from Roth IRAs after age 59½ are generally not taxed, as you make your contributions to a Roth with after-tax dollars. The Roth IRA has flexible withdrawal rules that allow you to take out contributions (but not earnings) for any reason without penalty or taxes. Once you reach age 59½ and have had the account open for five years, you can withdraw your earnings tax and penalty free.

RICK'S TIP: Taxpayers with income in excess of the phase-out levels may still be able to make Roth contributions by making a non-deductible IRA contribution and then converting it to a Roth. (I cover these conversions in more detail in the next section.)

The problem with the Roth IRA is meeting the eligibility rules to contribute money to it. These rules require you to have earned income—but not too much. In 2016, eligibility phases out for a joint filer with modified adjusted gross income (MAGI), between $184,000 and $194,000. For a single filer, the phase-out is between MAGI of $117,000 and $132,000. The contribution limits and phase-out levels are indexed to inflation after 2016, although the contribution levels will only increase in $1,000 increments. Like traditional IRAs, the Roth IRA allows 2016 contributions of $5,500 per person for those who qualify ($6,500 if you're age 50 or older at the end of the year).

Unlike with traditional IRAs, there are no age limits for making contributions to a Roth IRA. A taxpayer who still has earned income isn't allowed to make contributions to a traditional IRA once he or she reaches age 70½. However, the taxpayer can continue to make contributions to a Roth IRA (as long as he or she doesn't exceed the income limits mentioned). There are also no minimum distribution requirements at age 70½ for a Roth IRA. You can allow the money to continue to grow tax-free as long as you want.

An IRA account (traditional or Roth) is more flexible than a 401(k) and many other retirement plans. You can invest it in almost whatever you want, from stocks and mutual funds to bonds and real estate. This is a huge advantage when you are attempting to construct an efficient investment strategy.

Roth 401(k)s

Many employers are now offering Roth 401(k)s to their employees. As with Roth IRAs, there is no up-front tax deduction but withdrawals are tax-free in retirement if you meet the same rules as listed above. Big advantages of the Roth 401(k) over the Roth IRA are there are no income-eligibility limits and you can potentially make larger contributions. Like traditional 401(k)s, employees can contribute up to $18,000 in 2016, plus an extra $6,000 if they are 50 or older.

my RAs

In 2014, President Obama announced the creation of an additonal retirement account to help Americans save for retirement. The my RA (short for my retirement account) is targeted to Americans without access to an employer-sponsored retirement savings plan such as a 401(k) or 403(b). That includes roughly half of all workers and 75% of part-time workers. Having access to an employer plan does not exclude you from participating, but there are income restrictions.

Savers with an annual income in 2015 of less than $131,000 for individuals and $193,000 for couples are eligible to participate. Workers earning more than these limits are not be permitted to contribute to a my RA.

There are no fees, and workers can enroll in the program with a minimum contribution of $25 and add through automatic payroll deductions as low as $5 per pay. The account functions as a Roth IRA, which allows savers to invest after-tax dollars and withdraw the money in retirement tax-free. Like a traditional Roth account, savers are allowed to contribute up to $5,500 a year under current limits. Workers can keep the same *my* RA when changing jobs, and can also roll the balance over to a private-sector retirement account at any time.

Once a participant's account balance reaches $15,000, or the account has been open for 30 years, the participant must roll it over to a private sector Roth IRA, where the money can continue to grow tax-free. They will also be able to withdraw their contributions at any time without penalty. However, anyone who withdraws the interest earned in the account before reaching age 59 1/2 will get hit with taxes and a possible penalty, just like with a Roth IRA. Unlike traditional Roth IRAs, the accounts are invested solely in government savings bonds. The account balance will never decrease in value and it will earn the same interest rate as the Thrift Savings Plan's Government Securities Investment Fund that is offered to federal workers. That fund earned 2.04% in 2015 and it had an average annual return of 2.94% for the 10 years ending December 31, 2015.

Roth Accounts for Younger People

One of the smartest moves a younger person can make is to invest in a Roth IRA. A person who starts saving $5,500 per year in a Roth IRA at age 20 could have over $1 million at age 60 if it grows at 6.5% per year. Provided the investor has followed the rules, no taxes would be owed to the IRS on any of the funds upon withdrawal.

Many taxpayers, young and old, find it difficult to give up the immediate tax savings they receive if they chose to make a tradi-tional IRA contribution that is deductible. In the example above, if the same person contributed to a traditional IRA, the entire $1 million would be taxable upon withdrawal. About $50,000 in taxes would have been saved along the way, but more than $200,000 in taxes would be owed when withdrawn from the account.

RICK'S TIP: A taxpayer eligible for the saver's credit could shave as much as $2,000 off his or her tax bill ($4,000 if married filing jointly). This tax break is a credit rather than a deduction. Credits come into play after you calculate how much tax you owe the IRS and reduce your tax bill dollar for dollar. The actual credit amount depends on income, filing status, and the contribution amount to a retirement account.

As the example demonstrates, there's no doubt the Roth IRA is a better choice for a younger person. A Roth contribution is a great way to gift money to your children or grandchildren as long as they have earned income. In addition to the long-term, tax-free growth your gift would provide them, they may also qualify for the retirement savings tax credit.

Retirement Saver's Credit

As Table 3-1 indicates, basically, the lower the income, the bigger the credit. Contributions to traditional and Roth IRAs as well as to 401(k) plans count toward computing the credit. In the case of the 401(k), only the employee contributions count, not any matching amounts the company contributed. The retirement savings credit is only available if the person files his or her own return and isn't claimed as a dependent on another person's tax return.

Roth Accounts as You Approach Retirement

You may hear the argument that if you expect to be in a much lower tax bracket during retirement than you're in now, a tax-deductible IRA is a better deal than even a Roth IRA—especially if you are within a few years from retirement. Some advisers say a contribution

2016 Saver's Credit			
Credit Rate	Married Filing Jointly	Head of Household	All Other Filers
50% of your contribution	AGI not more than $37,000	AGI not more than $27,750	AGI not more than $18,500
20% of your contribution	$37,001– $40,000	$27,751–$30,000	$18,501– $20,000
10% of your contribution	$40,001– $61,500	$30,001–$46,125	$20,001– $30,750
0% of your contribution	More than $61,500	More than $46,125	More than $30,750

Source: IRS.gov

to a Roth must remain in the account for at least 10 years to make it worthwhile; otherwise, the contribution won't have enough time to accumulate tax-free to offset giving up the immediate benefit of the tax deduction. This would seem to make sense if you can take a tax deduction in the 25% tax bracket and expect to pay only 15% tax on the withdrawal.

However, there are a couple of fundamental problems with this philosophy. First, you're probably already over-weighted in tax-deferred accounts, as most people are at retirement. (That said, I'd be more inclined to go along with the philosophy if you're in the unusual position of having your New Three-Legged Stool over-weighted in favor of the Roth.) Second, it's unlikely you'll be withdrawing this money early in your retirement. The contributions would probably have a few years of earnings before withdrawal, and time is on the Roth IRA's side, because time helps the account through tax-free compounding.

Finally, you may retire to a lower tax bracket, but the taxation of Social Security benefits could put you into a higher "effective" tax rate. Social Security benefits aren't taxable until you reach a certain level of income. IRA distributions contribute to your income level and potentially make your Social Security benefits taxable. Let's assume you withdraw $1,000 from your IRA. The withdrawal causes $500 of your Social Security benefit to become taxable. You pay 15% on the amount of the IRA withdrawal and 15% on the taxable portion of your Social Security benefits, for a total tax of $225 ($1,000 + $500 × 15%). That's an effective tax rate of 22.5% on the IRA withdrawal. (For a complete explanation of the taxation of Social Security benefits, see Chapter 5.)

Roth IRA distributions don't add to the calculation for determining the taxation of Social Security benefits. This is also important for those who itemize deductions. Medical expenses and miscellaneous itemized deductions are both reduced by a percentage of your adjusted gross income. IRA distributions add to your adjusted gross income, which will reduce the amount of these deductions. Yet Roth IRA distributions don't add to adjusted gross income. Alternative minimum tax (AMT) is calculated using your net taxable income before personal exemptions, but Roth IRA distributions aren't part of the net taxable income.

Roth IRA Conversions: Better Than Any Tax Break

The changes to the nation's tax system President George W. Bush signed into law in May 2007 had a profound effect on the Roth IRA. A lot of attention at the time was focused on the amount of income exempted from the AMT, dividends, and capital gains. However, the Roth IRA conversion provision offered long-term benefits more valuable than any tax cut.

In 2010, eligibility to participate in the conversion provision was extended to include taxpayers with more than $100,000 in adjusted gross income. Converting an IRA to a Roth creates a taxable event on any amount of pre-tax money in the IRA. The tax is paid in the year of conversion, resulting in all the earnings growing tax-free from that point on (providing the rules are followed). You wouldn't be

---

Roth Accounts

- You should make a Roth contribution in any tax year you have earned income that doesn't exceed the income limits.
- Make non-deductible IRA contributions when your income exceeds the limits, with the goal of converting them to Roth IRAs.
- Both spouses can make Roth IRA contributions even if only one of them has earned income if the couple files a joint tax return.
- You can make a Roth IRA contribution after you turn 70½ as long as you or your spouse has earned income.

---

forced to withdraw funds at age 70½ and could subsequently pass the money to your heirs in a more tax-advantageous way. Why do this? Because you don't have to pay tax on the earnings in your Roth IRA account when you withdraw the money.

This provision has the potential to wield significant influence on the millions of Baby Boomers who make more than $100,000 a year. Some estimate a $6.4 billion income windfall to the government over 10 years as Baby Boomers convert and pay income taxes on money withdrawn from traditional IRAs (spent or converted, either way, the government collects).

Lifting the income limit on conversions opened the door for taxpayers exceeding the income limits for Roth contributions to make them through a two-step process. For 2016, the maximum contributions to a Roth IRA are limited to single taxpayers who make no more than $117,000 in adjusted gross income and to couples with a combined income of no more than $184,000. Partial contributions can be made for single filers with incomes between $117,000 and $132,000 and for joint filers with incomes between $184,000 and

$194,000. Those income limits are indexed for inflation. However, there is no income limit for making non-deductible contributions to a traditional IRA or converting an IRA to a Roth. The taxpayer makes a contribution to an IRA and then converts the entire amount to a Roth IRA.

The Pro-Rata Rule for Roth Conversions

Non-deductible contributions to an IRA represent after-tax money. Deductible contributions plus earnings in all IRA accounts represent pre-tax money. How these funds are accounted for in the event of a partial Roth conversion is referred to as the pro-rata rule.

The formula for the pro-rata calculation is: the total after-tax money in all IRAs divided by total value of all IRAs multiplied by the amount converted. Let's suppose that you made three $5,000 non-deductible contributions to an IRA over the past couple of years (a total of $15,000). That IRA is now worth $20,000, including growth. You also have an IRA rollover account that is worth $80,000.

When you convert the $20,000 IRA to a Roth, $3,000 will be con-sidered after-tax and $17,000 will be considered pre-tax ($100,000 ÷ $15,000 = 15%; $20,000 × 15% = 3,000). Even though you only made after-tax contributions to the $20,000 IRA, the IRS says you have to consider the value of all IRAs to determine the pro-rata portion that is after tax. In this example, the IRA rollover now has $12,000 in after-tax money.

To make things even trickier, you can't calculate the exact pro-rata percentage until the end of the year. The total value of your IRAs used in the pro-rata rule includes the account values as of December 31st of the year of conversion. Any growth (or loss) in the funds remain-ing in your IRA from time of conversion to the end of the year will have an impact on the pro-rata calculation. This is one reason I rec-ommend allocating fixed-income investments to an IRA and equity investments to a Roth IRA and taxable accounts. For most investors, the change in value will not be that significant, but it is an important detail to be aware of when planning your taxes.

A much more significant impact from this rule comes to those who decide to roll over a 401(k) or other type of company plan. Only the total value of IRA accounts is used in the pro-rata rule. 401(k), 403(b), and profit sharing plan values are not included in the pro-rata formula. The value of one of these type of accounts would be included if you decided to roll over the plan assets to an IRA during the year.

Let's go back to my example of the $20,000 Roth conversion. If you decided to roll over a $400,000 401(k) plan to an IRA in the same year as the conversion, the value of that plan will now be included in the formula. This results in only $600 of the $20,000 Roth conversion now being considered after-tax ($15,000 after-tax ÷ $500,000 total IRA assets = 3%; 3% times the $20,000 amount converted = $600). This is very important to keep in mind when doing a rollover in the same year as a Roth conversion if after-tax money is involved.

Finally, SEP IRA values and SIMPLE IRA values are included in the definition of all IRAs. Even though these types of accounts are company-sponsored they must be included in the pro-rata calculation.

Estate Planning and Roth IRAs

The Roth IRA's highest value could be in the estate-planning area. (Check out the "Estate Planning With a Roth IRA" section for extended detail on this subject. For now, I'll give you the short story.) If you are a high-net worth, self-employed person, you can move money from a "qualified" retirement savings plan such as a 401(k) into a Roth IRA. By paying income tax on your IRA funds in advance, the amount paid in income tax at the time of the conversion is removed from your estate as the IRA holder. This will potentially lower the amount of tax that will have to be paid on your estate. This avoids one of the problems the Richardson family, whom I talked about way back in the Introduction, ran into with their estate, when the amount of estate tax paid could not be used to completely offset the income tax.

Now you know the nuts and bolts behind Roth IRA conversions, how do you determine if this strategy is right for you? There's no easy answer to this question. Ultimately, each person must analyze this option based on his or her individual circumstances.

In general, **a conversion may be a good idea** if:

> **RICK'S TIP:** Beneficiaries of Roth IRAs must start taking distributions when they receive the accounts, but the distributions can be spread out over their life expectancies and the money is income tax-free when withdrawn.

- You don't plan to touch the money in the Roth for at least the next eight years.
- You can pay the income taxes due on the conversion without using funds from the traditional IRA when you convert.
- You expect to be in a higher tax bracket in future years. Paying the taxes now while you're in a lower income tax bracket should save you income taxes later.
- You don't expect to need the Roth IRA assets for income and want to build an estate for your heirs. In this case, the Roth IRA can minimize the overall income tax burden to the family; heirs get the proceeds free of income taxes, and in the interim, the proceeds can continue growing tax-free.
- You don't expect to need income from your IRA, and you wish to avoid the annual mandatory distributions required from a traditional IRA when you reach age 70½.
- You believe current income tax rates are at the lowest level we'll ever see and Congress will most likely increase tax rates in the years to come.

A conversion is generally a bad idea if:

- You can't pay the income taxes due on the conversion without using funds from the traditional IRA. Taking the tax from the conversion assets reduces the amount within the Roth for compounding purposes. An early withdrawal penalty may apply for taking money from a traditional IRA before age 59½.
- The added income for the year caused by the conversion puts you in a significantly higher tax bracket. (To avoid this, you can have your tax adviser calculate the amount of income you can add before moving into the next higher bracket, then only convert the amount that keeps you in your current tax bracket.)
- You expect to be in a lower tax bracket in future years. Paying the taxes later at the lower rate would offset the lack of tax-free growth.
- You think Congress will adopt a radical change in the tax system whereby income will no longer be taxed. A national sales tax or some form of value added tax has been debated for years. Obviously, it wouldn't make sense to pay tax on income now if the income tax will be abolished in the future.

Convert to Roth in Down Markets

The stock market meltdown from 2008 to 2009 caused many investors to lose faith in the financial markets, with good reason: The Dow Jones Industrial Average fell 54% from its peak in October 2007 to its low in March 2009. But for long-term investors holding stocks and stock funds in their retirement accounts, this was the perfect opportunity for a Roth conversion.

You'll have to pay taxes on the money you withdraw from your IRA account someday; what better time than when the market is

> **RICK'S TIP:** You may want to use some of the online calculators to help with your conversion decision. *Bankrate.com* has a Roth conversion calculator that is free and easy to use. Fidelity Investments also has a Roth conversion evaluator online that takes you through the process.

down and you can pay tax on the discounted value? This strategy calls for some advance tax planning so you know how much tax you will owe on a conversion. Then, when the stock market goes into one of its sell-off periods, you'll be able to convert at the lower account value. If you're doing a partial conversion, you'll be able to convert more shares.

The big advantage of the Roth conversion strategy comes when the market recovers and the account grows back to its original value, because the account growth from the recovery will be all tax-free (at least, it will be once you hold the funds for five years and have reached age 59½)! Check out the advantages of this strategy enjoyed by one of my clients, Jim Haller.

CASE STUDY

Jim Haller, investor

Jim Haller was still five years from retirement when the stock market dropped in 2008–2009. He'd watched his retirement accounts slip from $1,000,000 at the beginning of 2008 to $750,000 in early 2009. His accounts were balanced between stocks and bonds; though the bonds helped offset some of the losses in the stocks, the IRA was still down 25% overall.

Like a lot of investors, Jim was over weighted in tax-deferred accounts. Most of his new savings were going into the 401(k) at work, which only added to his lop-sided savings. Now was the time to act if he was going to have any chance of obtaining a balanced Three-Legged Stool for retirement.

After we ran some tax calculations, Jim determined he could afford to pay the tax on a partial Roth conversion of $100,000. We chose only the stocks in his IRA to convert to the Roth and completed the conversion in 2009. The stock market had already started to recover when Jim was preparing to file his taxes in 2010. But what if the market had not recovered? What if we miscalculated the cost of the conversion? Jim still had the option of "recharacterizing" the Roth conversion before his filing deadline.

If Jim had recharacterized, there would have been no tax due on the conversion. If he'd recharacterized later in the year but before October 15, he would file an amended tax return to get back the taxes he paid on the value of the conversion (this must be done for state tax returns as well). Another circumstance in which tax payers recharacterize a conversion is when they find the value they converted and paid tax on has declined due to a stock market drop. This could happen when a stock market downturn occurs early in the year.

RICK'S TIP: The process of undoing a Roth conversion is called a Roth recharacterization. The IRS says it can be done until October 15 of the year following the year of the conversion. This rule exists because tax payers often don't know what their total income will be until after the end of the tax year. A recharacterization allows you to put the money back into an IRA without paying tax or penalty. To recharacterize, the taxpayer must make a direct transfer of the funds from the Roth IRA back to a traditional IRA. The Roth conversion is now treated as though it never happened.

Jim paid the tax on his conversion. As it turned out, he ended up with a half-price sale. Five years later, the $100,000 Roth was worth $156,000. All of the growth he reclaimed was tax-free, and, best of all, any future earnings would be tax-exempt, too.

Fortunately, 54% drops in the stock market like the one from 2008 to 2009 are rare. However, 10–20% drops are a more common part of the stock market cycle. So when you hear the newscasters say "correction," think "conversion," because that means the stocks in your IRA are at a discount—and you should take advantage of it.

Roth IRA Conversions

- Anyone can convert an IRA to a Roth. There are no income limitations.
- The conversion will provide you with more flexible distribution capabilities since you can—but won't be forced to—start withdrawing money five years after it has been in the Roth.
- Before you convert an IRA to a Roth, make sure you know how much it will cost in taxes. You should have the money to pay the taxes in an account outside of the Roth.
- Amateurs fear stock market corrections and try to time the market to avoid them. They usually end up buying high and selling low. Pros know corrections are part of the stock market's normal trading pattern and use them to take advantage of opportunities.

Read This *Before* You Roll Over Your Company-Sponsored Plan!

The IRS handed us another tool in 2014 to use for building Roth IRAs. A new IRS ruling provides a path for rolling over any after-tax money in an employer-sponsored plan, such as 401(k)s and 403(b)s, to a Roth IRA. Employees with after-tax money in these plans can take a complete distribution and direct the plan administrator to send pre-tax dollars to a traditional IRA or another plan and then roll the after-tax contributions into a Roth IRA tax-free.

Rolling after-tax money in an employer plan to a Roth has been an area of uncertainty among tax professionals and financial planners because of the pro-rata rule. This rule applies to non-deductible contributions in a traditional IRA. Distributions from an IRA that contains both pre-tax dollars (deductible contributions and earnings) and after-tax dollars (non-deductible contributions) must be allocated pro-rata to determine the taxable amount of the distribution.

The IRS was never clear on whether the pro-rata rule would apply to distributions from an employer-sponsored plan. Many financial advisers didn't want to take the risk of separating after-tax money during a rollover and move it into a Roth. However, it is possible to separate after-tax money and have the employer plan send a check for the after-tax portion to the participant. The fact that this can now be deposited directly to a Roth was finally made clear in the latest ruling.

There are a few rules to follow to do the transaction properly. The transfer of after-tax and pre-tax money must be done at the same time. Also, the taxpayer must instruct the plan administrator that the after-tax money is to be sent to a different account.

High-income taxpayers now have a way to get money into a Roth IRA without choosing the Roth 401(k) option. Only married taxpayers with a combined adjusted gross income (AGI) below $181,000 and singles with AGIs less than $114,000 can contribute up to $5,500 to a

Roth IRA—$6,500 if they are age 50 and older in 2016. The amount of contributions are phased out until no contributions are permitted when AGI tops $191,000 (joint filers) or $129,000 (single filers).

Taxpayers with AGI above these levels cannot contribute to a Roth unless they make non-deductible contributions and convert them to a Roth. This may not be feasible if they already have pre-tax money in IRA accounts due to the pro-rata rule. The other option could be contributing to a Roth 401(k). However, this option would take away from the amount they can contribute pre-tax which reduces current tax liability.

Now, upper income taxpayers can build a Roth IRA by making after-tax contributions to their employer plan and separating these contributions to a Roth when they roll over the account. Making after-tax contributions for a number of years before retirement could build a sizeable Roth IRA providing a source of tax-free income.

In order to implement this strategy, your employer may have to amend the plan to accept after-tax contributions if they are not allowed currently. There is a $53,000 ceiling in 2016 ($59,000 if 50 or older) on the amount of total contributions that can be made to a retirement plan on a worker's behalf. Employer and employee contributions count toward the cap.

Taxpayers will want to make the maximum pre-tax contributions first ($18,000 or $24,000 if age 50 or older in 2016).

Let's say a taxpayer over age 50 contributes the $24,000 maximum 401(k) contribution and their employer adds $5,000. In this example, this person could make up to $30,000 of after-tax additions to their plan. Anyone considering this strategy should check with their plan administrator to make sure top-heavy testing doesn't place further restrictions on the amount a highly compensated employee can contribute to the plan.

Unfortunately, the new ruling doesn't change the pro-rata rule for non-deductible contributions made to a traditional IRA. Taxpayers won't be able to segregate just the non-deductible contributions and roll them tax-free into a Roth.

———

Our discussion about how to keep the IRS away from your retirement has now come full circle. With the knowledge you've gained about pre-tax, after-tax, and tax-free retirement savings strategies, you're well on your way toward establishing a personal plan that will keep you and your family comfortable long after you retire. In the next chapter, I'll tell you how to structure your plan so it strikes a good balance between these three strategies. We'll also talk about the most tax-efficient ways to withdraw your retirement savings when it finally comes time to reap the rewards you've worked so hard to build. Finally, I'll give you tips on how to choose a smart financial adviser to help guide you through it all.

CHAPTER 4

Distributions: Strike an Ideal Balance Among All of Your Accounts

The Retirement Distribution (R/D) Factor

As we've discussed throughout this book, the New Three-Legged Stool approach to retirement is based on balancing your savings among tax-deferred, after-tax, and tax-free accounts. Many people today, unwisely, aren't concerned with balancing their savings. They simply save money in their company's 401(k) and spend everything else. When these people enter retirement, they'll have nothing but their tax-deferred savings to draw upon.

I believe we are approaching a time when the IRS will be even more aggressive in taxing these assets. Aggressive taxation goes against what we were originally told; IRA and 401(k) accounts were created so we could defer income now until we retire and enter a *lower* tax bracket! It's likely just the opposite will happen: We may be seeing the lowest tax brackets *now*. The growing national debt and retiring Baby Boomers will probably put a greater strain on government finances in the future.

By determining your R/D Factor now, you can help ensure you don't end up like the countless retirees who didn't balance their savings and pay the price in additional taxes. The R/D Factor is a measure of how well you've done with reducing your taxable retirement income by building a balanced Three-Legged Stool. The scale runs from 0, the point at which all of your income is taxable, to 100, where all of your retirement income is tax-free. After you determine your R/D Factor, you can use it to create a balanced retirement plan if you don't already have one, or to rebalance your existing plan to ensure it will be tax efficient upon your retirement.

The following example of my clients John and Mary Pritchard will give you an idea of how the R/D Factor works.

CASE STUDY
John and Mary Pritchard, future retirees

John and Mary Pritchard have done what they think is a perfect job of saving for retirement by completely balancing their savings. By the time they retire, they expect to have $1 million in tax-deferred IRA/401(k) accounts; $1 million in their joint after-tax account; and $1 million in their Roth IRA tax-free accounts. Their total retirement savings of $3 million is projected to distribute 4% ($120,000) per year based on the Trinity Study (more detail on this study later in the chapter).

To calculate the R/D Factor for the Pritchards, we assume one-third of their income will be drawn from each of the three sources, as shown in Table 4-1.

Account Type	Total Income	Non-Taxable Portion	R/D Factor
Tax-Deferred Account	$40,000	$0	0
After-Tax Account	$40,000	$10,000	25
Tax-Free Account	$40,000	$40,000	100
Total	**$120,000**	**$50,000**	**42**

Note the tax liability from the after-tax account isn't necessarily based on the amount of the withdrawal. The earnings in the after-tax account won't be taxed based on whether they're withdrawn or not. To estimate this amount, we assume the Pritchards have followed the allocation strategy explained in Leg Two of this book and only have stock funds in the after-tax account.

Even after following all the tax-efficient strategies I've explained in the book, there will be some tax implications from dividend distributions and rebalancing. A reasonable assumption is that one-third of the return will be taxable each year. Assuming the after-tax accounts average 9%, then 3%, or $30,000, of their return will be taxable.

The Pritchards will be left with $70,000 in taxable income to report. If this was their only taxable income in 2016 and they filed a joint return, claiming only the standard deduction ($12,600) and personal exemptions ($4,050 each), they'd owe tax on $49,350. This amount would put them in the 15% bracket. The earnings in their taxable account would be qualified dividends and long-term capital gains taxed at 0%. Only the distribution from the tax deferred account would have tax implications. Their total tax bill would be about $2,000 on $120,000 of income. Not bad!

The R/D Factor for the Pritchards is 42 in this example, since 42% of their retirement income will be non-taxable. When they retire, they can adjust this factor if they want by changing the amount they distribute from the three accounts. This offers a lot of flexibility until they reach the age of 70½ and must start taking minimum distributions from the tax-deferred accounts.

You should work with a knowledgeable tax adviser to develop strategies to use the R/D Factor to your advantage. In the example, the Pritchards may want to withdraw more from the tax-deferred accounts when they retire in order to maximize the 15% bracket. (The 2016 threshold for married filing jointly is $75,300 in taxable income.) And once they start drawing Social Security, they may want to increase their R/D Factor by taking more from the after-tax and tax-free accounts to minimize the amount of Social Security benefits that are taxed. (I explain this strategy in more detail in Chapter 5.)

RICK'S TIP: A realistic objective is to aim for an R/D Factor of 40–50. This would provide a balance between tax planning today and saving for retirement in the future.

Why not 100?

The New Three-Legged Stool approach to retirement planning is all about balance. Whenever I explain the strategy to audiences, someone usually asks me why we don't try to save everything in the tax-free accounts. Good question! True, saving everything in tax-free accounts would give you an R/D Factor of 100, and you wouldn't have to worry about income taxes in retirement. But there's a two-fold problem with making 100% tax-free savings your goal:

1. There are immediate tax benefits to using IRA and 401(k) accounts you don't want to ignore. Annual tax planning should take into consideration the level of pre-tax savings that will keep you in a lower tax bracket. Itemized deductions are reduced on your total adjusted gross income (AGI). Alternative minimum tax (AMT) calculations are also based on your AGI. Pre-tax savings accounts are often the only tool we have to minimize the AMT burden.

2. As you know from reading about Leg Three in Chapter 3, there are limits to putting money into a Roth IRA. Unless you have a Roth 401(k) offered through your employer, you may only be able to contribute to a Roth using the two-step approach of non-deductible IRA contributions first. Even using these strategies, it would still be difficult to put 100% of retirement savings into a Roth without ignoring some significant tax issues.

The R/D Factor

The R/D Factor is the percentage of your retirement income that won't be taxable. Ideally, you should shoot for an R/D Factor of 40–50.

When you retire, you should continue to manage your R/D Factor to take maximum advantage of your tax situation each year, accelerating taxable income in low tax years and minimizing taxable income when needed to stay in a lower tax bracket.

Balance is the goal. Don't neglect to do tax planning today for a tax-free retirement later. Because tax laws change frequently, you want to take advantage of tax incentives now, as they may not be there down the road.

How and When to Take Retirement Savings Distributions

When it finally comes time to begin taking distributions from your retirement savings accounts, you'll be in an ideal position—because you'll have balanced all of your accounts around your R/D Factor you determined long ago. The general rule of thumb about distributions is to withdraw money from your retirement accounts in the following order:

1. Taxable accounts (stocks and mutual funds).
2. Tax-deferred accounts (traditional IRAs and qualified plans).
3. Tax-free accounts (Roth IRAs).

The logic behind this order is this: Because you already paid taxes on the earnings from taxable accounts, there's no increased tax burden for spending the dividends and capital gains distributions. Therefore, withdraw from taxable accounts first.

The way distributions are taken from each of these accounts, and the way those distributions are taxed, are both determined by age and investment type. First, let's talk about the two IRS-approved ways for calculating the annual distribution amount from an IRA.

RICK'S TIP: When determining the taxes on capital gains, remember assets held longer than one year in taxable accounts are subject to the long-term capital gains rate, which is a maximum of 15% (20% for the top tax bracket). Tax-deferred account distributions are treated as ordinary income and are subject to rates of up to 39.6%. Obviously, you should keep your assets in tax-free or tax-advantaged accounts as long as possible, because they continue to grow tax-deferred and potentially faster than a comparable investment in a taxable account.

1. Required Minimum Distribution (RMD)

RMD payments are calculated by dividing the account balance at the end of the year by the appropriate life-expectancy factor from one of three IRS life-expectancy tables: Uniform Lifetime, Single Life, or Joint and Last Survivor. To find the current RMD, divide the adjusted balance of all of your IRAs on December 31st of the previous year by the applicable divisor from the IRS Uniform Lifetime Table (Table 4-2, which you can also find at *www.irs.gov*). Be sure to use the age you'll be on the current year's birthday. For example, if Joe turns 73 in December, find 73 on the table and use the appropriate factor to calculate his RMD—in this case, 24.7.

If your spouse is the sole beneficiary of the IRA and is more than 10 years younger than you, you may use a separate IRS table—Joint and Last Survivor—which addresses actual joint life expectancy and will result in a lower RMD. If you die before the account is depleted, it will be passed to your designated beneficiary.

2. 72(t) payments

- Section 72(t) of the Internal Revenue Code, which imposes the 10% early withdrawal penalty on IRAs, also allows specific types of penalty-free distributions— known as a series of substantially equal payments or 72(t) payments—prior to age 59½.
- According to IRS rules, once the 72(t) payments have begun, no contributions, transfers, or rollovers into the

RICK'S TIP: Keep in mind once you start taking RMDs from retirement accounts, you can alter the distribution strategy accordingly, taking less from taxable accounts. You may also be able to stop paying estimated tax payments by electing to have taxes withheld from your RMD.

Age	Applicable Divisor	Age	Applicable Divisor	Age	Applicable Divisor
70	27.4	86	14.1	102	5.5
71	26.5	87	13.4	103	5.2
72	25.6	88	12.7	104	4.9
73	24.7	89	12	105	4.5
74	23.8	90	11.4	106	4.2
75	22.9	91	10.8	107	3.9
76	22	92	10.2	108	3.7
77	21.3	93	9.6	109	3.4
78	20.3	94	9.1	110	3.1
79	19.5	95	8.6	111	2.9
80	18.7	96	8.1	112	2.6
81	17.9	97	7.6	113	2.4
82	17.1	98	7.1	114	2.1
83	16.3	99	6.7	115+	1.9
84	15.5	100	6.3		
85	14.8	101	5.9		

IRA are permitted, and the 72(t) payment stream can't be modified (except for the one-time election to the RMD method discussed above). Any other modification would result in a 10% penalty, plus interest, on all payments made from the account to date.

- If an investor needs to roll money into an IRA but has already begun 72(t) payments, a new IRA must be opened.

The following is a breakdown of what will happen to each of your accounts should you attempt to withdraw money at certain ages.

IRA Distribution Age: Younger Than 59½

Unforeseen circumstances sometimes force you to dip into your retirement savings before the standard retirement age of 59½. Should you decide to take retirement distributions before this age, the withdrawals will be considered "premature" and will be subject to certain penalties according to the account type.

TRADITIONAL AND SEP IRAS

If you are younger than 59½, distributions from a traditional or Simplified Employee Pension (SEP) IRA are considered premature distributions and subject to ordinary income tax and a 10% penalty. However, there are exceptions to the 10% penalty, including:

- Rollover within 60 days.
- Death.
- Permanent disability as defined by the Internal Revenue Code.
- Unreimbursed medical expenses in excess of 10% of your adjusted gross income.
- Qualified higher education expenses.
- Purchase, building, or rebuilding of a first home ($10,000 lifetime limit).
- Payment of medical insurance during a period in which you received unemployment compensation for at least 12 weeks.
- Distributions from an inherited IRA.
- An IRS levy.
- Distributions taken as a series of substantially equal periodic payments (72(t) payments, described above).

SIMPLE IRAs

Savings Incentive Match Plan for Employees (SIMPLE) IRAs follow the same rules as traditional and SEP IRAs. However, during the first two years a SIMPLE IRA is open: Any premature distribution that doesn't qualify for one of the exceptions is subject to a 25% penalty, rather than 10%; and it can only be rolled into another SIMPLE IRA, in which case, it will continue to be tax deferred.

Roth IRAs

Although investors may withdraw their contributions at any time without tax or penalty prior to age 59½, distribution of earnings is considered premature and is subject to a 10% penalty. Exceptions to the 10% penalty include:

- Unreimbursed medical expenses in excess of 10% of your adjusted gross income.
- Qualified higher education expenses.
- Payment of medical insurance during a period in which you received unemployment compensation for at least 12 weeks.
- Distributions from an inherited IRA.
- An IRS levy.
- Distributions taken as a series of substantially equal periodic payments (72(t) payments).

Additionally, any earnings distributed from the account before it is five years old are subject to ordinary income tax. There are exceptions to both, however, including:

- Rollover within 60 days.
- Death.
- Permanent disability as defined by the Internal Revenue Code.

- Purchase, building, or rebuilding of a first home ($10,000 lifetime limit).

(See the forthcoming section "Tips for Taking an Early Retirement" to find out more about how to maximize distributions before age 59½.)

IRA Distribution Age: 59½ to 70½

At age 59½, distributions become qualified—that is, no longer subject to the 10% premature distribution penalty. However, it is still important to understand the tax consequences of different IRA distributions.

TRADITIONAL, SEP, AND SIMPLE IRAS

When you reach age 59½, distributions aren't penalized but may be taxed as ordinary income. If you've made both deductible and non-deductible contributions to an IRA, the IRS will consider each distribution to be partially taxable and partially tax-free. IRS Form 8606 provides instructions for calculating the taxable portion. (See the explanation of the pro-rata rule in Chapter 3.)

ROTH IRAS

Qualified distributions from a Roth IRA are those made after the five-year period beginning with the year the first contribution was made and that meet one of the following criteria:

- The Roth IRA owner is age 59½.
- The Roth IRA owner is disabled.
- Payment is made to a beneficiary after the Roth IRA owner's death.
- The Roth IRA owner is buying, building, or rebuilding a first home ($10,000 lifetime limit).

IRA Distribution Age: 70½ or Older

At 70½ years of age and older, distributions become required. The IRS forces IRA owners to begin taking distributions or suffer the tax consequences, which break down as follows:

TRADITIONAL, SEP, AND SIMPLE IRAS

Tax laws require minimum distributions from an IRA begin no later than the required beginning date (RBD), or April 1 following the calendar year in which the IRA owner turns 70½. For example, if Alice turned 70 on March 12, 2005, (therefore 70½ six months later on September 12), she must take her first required minimum distribution (RMD) no later than April 1, 2006. The April 1 rule is applicable only in the first year in which an RMD must be taken. In subsequent years, the deadline is December 31. Most people opt to take their first RMD by December 31 of the year they turn 70½ to avoid two taxable distributions in the same year. Returning to our example, if Alice waits until April 1, 2006, to take her first RMD, she'll have to take another minimum distribution by December 31, 2006, and both will be reported on her 2006 tax return. Failure to take any year's RMD will result in a 50% penalty on the amount that should have been withdrawn.

ROTH IRAS

There are no required minimum distributions from Roth IRAs. However, your heirs will be required to make withdrawals upon your death.

Special Circumstances for Inherited IRAs

If you inherit an IRA, the account will be subject to different tax rules depending on whether the original owner passed away before or after the required beginning date (RBD) for taking distributions.

If the **IRA owner passes away before the RBD,** the inherited IRA rules are:

Spouse Beneficiary

- Roll over the assets to his or her own IRA and assume ownership of them. He or she will then be subject to any applicable withdrawal penalties, including premature distribution penalties.
- Deplete the balance of the account by the end of the fifth year following the IRA owner's death.
- Take annual distributions based on his or her own life-expectancy factor as determined by the IRS Single Life table.
- Wait until the deceased would've reached his or her RBD, and then begin taking distributions based on the surviving spouse's life-expectancy factor.

Non-Spouse Beneficiary

- Deplete the balance of the account by the end of the fifth year following the IRA owner's death.
- Take annual distributions based on his or her own life-expectancy factor. Distributions must start in the year following the IRA owner's year of death. In subsequent years, the minimum distribution will be determined by the previous year's factor minus one.

Non-Individual Beneficiary

- Deplete the balance of the account by the end of the fifth year following the IRA owner's death.

The following rules apply if the **IRA owner passes away after the RBD.**

Spouse Beneficiary

- Roll over the assets to his or her own IRA and assume ownership of them. Take annual distributions based on his or her life-expectancy factor.

Non-Spouse Beneficiary

- Take annual distributions based on his or her life-expectancy factor. Distributions must start in the year following the IRA owner's year of death. In subsequent years, the minimum distribution will be determined by the previous year's factor minus one.

Non-Individual Beneficiary

- Take annual distributions based on the deceased's life-expectancy factor at death minus one—subtracting one for each subsequent year.

Distributions From Qualified Plans

To recap, distributions become qualified at age 59½, meaning they are no longer subject to the 10% premature distribution penalty. Though all qualified plans must follow some basic rules set forth by the Employee Retirement Income Security Act (ERISA), many plans are customized. The following information is a general overview of distributions from qualified plans. If you are considering a qualified plan, be sure to ask for the Summary Plan Description (SPD) and study the distribution rules carefully.

As I did with IRA distributions, I've broken down the consequences of withdrawing money from qualified plans at various ages.

Qualified Plan Distribution Age: Younger Than 59½

Taking distributions from a qualified plan before age 59½ makes those distributions premature. Distributions made prior to age 59½ that aren't rolled over to another plan are generally subject to a 10% penalty. However, there are exceptions, which include:

- Death.
- Permanent disability as defined by the Internal Revenue Code.
- Attainment of age 55 and separation from service.
- Unreimbursed medical expenses in excess of 10% of your adjusted gross income.
- Distributions made to a former spouse pursuant to a qualified domestic relations order.
- 72(t) payments.
- Financial hardship (if permitted by the plan).
- Plan termination without a successor plan named.
- RMDs.

Qualified Plan Distribution Age: 59½ and Older

Distributions of elective deferrals are considered qualified after age 59½. Therefore, these distributions would be subject to ordinary income tax but no penalty.

Qualified Plan Distribution Age: 70½ and Older

In general, the same RMD rules that apply to IRAs apply to qualified plans.

Distributions Eligible for Rollover

Whether they come from an IRA or qualified plan, all distributions are eligible to roll over to another plan or IRA, except:

- Hardship withdrawals (when permitted by the plan).
- RMDs.
- 72(t) payments after separation from service.

Plans are required to withhold 20% from eligible rollover distributions that are not directly rolled into a qualified receiving account. If a participant receives a distribution check and then decides to roll it into another plan, he or she must deposit the check into the new plan or IRA within 60 days of receiving it. To avoid taxes and penalties, the participant must pay out of pocket the amount of the 20% withheld by the plan before depositing the check. If not, the 20% will be subject to income tax—and a 10% penalty if the participant isn't yet 59½.

For example, John, a retiree, takes a $100,000 distribution from his former employer's 401(k) and requests the check be sent directly to him. The plan must withhold 20% and send John a check for $80,000. If he then decides to roll his money into an IRA, he must contribute $20,000 of his own funds to make up the amount withheld by his former employer. Otherwise, that $20,000 will be subject to income tax and, if John is younger than 59½, a 10% premature distribution penalty.

Other Distribution Exceptions

In addition to the exceptions I've mentioned, there are two other circumstances in which you may be permitted to take distributions without penalty.

IN-SERVICE WITHDRAWALS

Certain plans may allow participants to take distributions before they've experienced a triggering event, which is often called an "in-service withdrawal." Some plans may limit the availability of these in-service withdrawals to instances of financial hardship, while others may be more flexible in their requirements. Check the plan's SPD to determine if in-service withdrawals are permitted.

LOANS

Some plans allow loans. The rules vary greatly from plan to plan, but in general, loans must not exceed 50% of the participant's vested balance or $50,000. The loan must generally be repaid in five years with at least quarterly payments. Longer repayment periods are allowed for loans used to purchase a primary residence.

Annual Withdrawal Rates: How Much Can You Afford?

You've spent years focusing on putting money into retirement savings, so you may not have given a lot of thought to taking money out when you retire. But spending your nest egg requires careful planning. Withdrawing too little money may mean you'll have to give up the lifestyle you were accustomed to before retirement. Taking out too much may deplete your savings too soon. So, how do you determine the withdrawal rate that works for you?

Before you answer this question, you should understand a few things:

- Both your withdrawal rate and your portfolio composition will have a significant impact on the longevity of your retirement savings.
- More conservative portfolios (those with 75–100% bonds) have not historically supported large withdrawal rates.
- The age at which you retire and your lifestyle in retirement should be considered when determining your withdrawal rate.
- Keep in mind you'll be required to begin taking distributions from most retirement plans once you reach age 70½.

Finding the Right Rate

In 1997, two economists at Trinity University in San Antonio, Texas, published a study in which they examined the probability of outliving savings. They based it on different withdrawal rates and different portfolio compositions over time. The results became known as the Trinity Study, which showed the critical factors affecting your savings are your asset allocation and your withdrawal rate. Table 4-3 is an updated version of that study.

The percentages listed represent your chances of running out of money based on asset allocation and annual withdrawal rates. The results are historical, from December 31, 1925, to December 31, 2004 (note past performance can't guarantee comparable future results, and historically, stocks are riskier investments than bonds).

Here's an example of how to use this information: If you had a portfolio with 75% stocks and 25% bonds, and you annually withdrew 7% of the initial value of the portfolio, there'd be a 5% chance

Portfolio Success Rates Inflation-Adjusted Withdrawals for Various Withdrawal Rates, Asset Allocations, and Retirement Durations Using Ibbotson's *Stocks, Bonds, Bills, and Inflation* Data, 1926–2015, S&P 500 and Intermediate-Term Government Bonds								
	3%	4%	5%	6%	7%	8%	9%	10%
100% Stocks								
15 Years	100	100	100	89	79	70	67	55
20 Years	100	100	92	82	72	63	49	41
25 Years	100	98	82	71	62	53	41	29
30 Years	100	93	77	66	54	41	36	21
35 Years	100	91	75	57	50	34	23	11
40 Years	100	88	69	53	37	29	22	10

75% Stocks								
15 Years	100	100	100	97	82	72	61	49
20 Years	100	100	94	80	69	55	46	27
25 Years	100	100	83	68	58	45	29	12
30 Years	100	98	77	57	46	34	13	3
35 Years	100	93	68	54	36	23	2	0
40 Years	100	92	65	43	29	6	2	0
50% Stocks								
15 Years	100	100	100	100	84	71	51	37
20 Years	100	100	99	79	62	42	28	6
25 Years	100	100	85	59	42	23	8	2
30 Years	100	100	69	44	23	10	2	0
35 Years	100	96	57	32	5	2	0	0
40 Years	100	86	43	16	0	0	0	0
25% Stocks								
15 Years	100	100	100	99	76	59	39	20
20 Years	100	100	94	63	46	23	8	1
25 Years	100	100	65	44	23	9	2	0
30 Years	100	87	43	18	10	3	0	0
35 Years	100	70	20	5	4	0	0	0
40 Years	98	43	8	0	0	0	0	0
0% Stocks								
15 Years	100	100	99	89	63	39	24	13
20 Years	100	94	76	39	27	11	3	0
25 Years	97	79	36	26	9	3	0	0
30 Years	82	43	20	10	3	0	0	0
35 Years	71	25	5	4	0	0	0	0
40 Years	61	8	0	0	0	0	0	0
Source: Wade Pfau, www.RetirementResearcher.com								

you'd run out of money in 20 years and a 10% chance you'd run out of money in 30 years.

The 4% Prudent Withdrawal Rule

The yield on fixed income is near record lows, while at the same time, the stock market has had two significant selloffs in the last 15 years. Many economists are predicting that we may be facing a time of increasing inflation.

Such a scenario is leading some Baby Boomers to wonder how much they will be able to withdraw from their retirement portfolios. Nearly 20 years ago, Financial Planner William Bengen considered this same question. His study on the returns for stocks and bonds going back to 1926 attempted to determine what rate of withdrawal could be sustained through 30 years of retirement. He published his study in 1994, concluding that a first-year withdrawal of 4% that was adjusted each subsequent year by the rate of inflation was sustainable.[1]

The study became widely known as "The 4% Rule." Bengen followed up his research by adding additional asset classes and concluded in a later study that the actual sustainable-withdrawal rate was 4.5%.[2] Subsequently, professors at Trinity University picked up on the research and examined various combinations of stocks and bonds with different withdrawal rates. Many retirement planners use Trinity Study research as the basis of their asset-allocation recommendations.[3]

Considering the low investment returns of the past decade, is this research still a valid basis for retirement plans in 2016? Mr. Bengen recently updated his research to try to answer this question. The worst-case scenario with a completed 30-year period would have been the person who retired at the beginning of 1969; the 1970s began with a devastating bear market that didn't end until 1982. Starting with a 4.5% distribution in the first year, the retiree's withdrawals would have reached a peak of 12.5% of principal before the bull market took off in the 1980s. Mr. Bengen concluded: "The damage done in the first 12 years, primarily from high inflation, was irreversible."[4] Using the 4.5% initial-withdrawal rate, the 1969 to 2000 portfolio was the only one of the 57 periods of 30 years to exhaust itself.

Is this period comparable to the last decade? The retiree who began his or her withdrawals at the beginning of 2000 faced an equally devastating bear market for the first three years, followed by an unprecedented second bear market in the 2008 financial crisis. However, inflation was relatively tame during the past decade, so the highest withdrawal rate only reached 5.9%—less than half of the peak for the 1969 retiree. It would appear that the 2000 retiree still has a good chance of sustaining another 15 years of withdrawals from his or her portfolio.

The challenge for the 2000 retiree is not the beginning years, but what the next 15 years of retirement bring in terms of investment results. If stock-market returns revert back to their historic average of 10% per year and inflation remains in check, the sustainability of the 4.5% withdrawal rate will hold. However, that is a question no one can answer.

We can learn some valuable lessons from the 1969 retiree scenario. Allowing the annual withdrawal rate to reach 12.5% caused too much principal to disappear before the great bull market of the 1980s got underway. My counsel to retirees is to never let annual withdrawals exceed 6% of their principal. Small reductions in spending can go a long way toward assuring that your principal stays intact for the long run.

Another approach is to begin with a smaller initial withdrawal. We prefer keeping it to 4% at the beginning of retirement. The smaller initial withdrawal gives you greater flexibility and room for a market decline without the need to reduce spending to stay below the 6% maximum level. Dimensional Funds' research shows that the worst one-year period for a 60% stock/40% bond portfolio was the period March 2008 to February 2009, which resulted in a loss of 32.1%. A retiree who began distributions at the beginning of this period would have a distribution rate of 5.9% at the beginning of the second year. No reductions would have been needed.[5]

No one knows what the future holds for the stock market. Many argue that today, the S&P 500 Index is fairly valued or even "cheap" by historical standards. The earnings on the companies in the S&P 500 have nearly doubled over the past 10 years, while the index itself has barely moved. The dividend yield for the index is more than a half-percent above the yield on the 10-year Treasury, which is unprecedented. A bull market like we had from 1982 to 1999 may be just waiting to take off, but many investors will be reluctant to take a big position in stocks after the two bear markets they suffered through in the last decade.

In summary, the 4% rule appears to be working for now. The key to your success in retirement will be to remain vigilant of your withdrawal rate in down markets and disciplined with your spending when you need to be. Put off big expenditures when you can until the money has already been earned during a good market. Stick to your investment strategy and don't let any current investment fads lead you astray.

Although asset allocation and withdrawal rates are important factors in retirement income planning, you'll also want to keep the following in mind:

- **Age at retirement:** Early retirement means your savings must last longer. In addition, your annual Social Security benefit will be reduced if you begin collecting before the full-benefit age, which gradually increases to age 67 over the next few years.
- **Lifestyle:** Do you plan to maintain your current lifestyle in retirement? If so, you'll likely need about 70 to 80% of your current income. But every situation is different. Be realistic about your expenses.
- **Required minimum distributions (RMDs):** As you well know by this point in the book, most retirement plans

RICK'S TIP: Remember: Seeking the advice of a good financial adviser will help you determine the asset allocation and withdrawal rates that best suit your financial needs.

require you begin taking minimum distributions at age 70½. You'll need to determine the required amount of the distribution you must take from your tax-deferred retirement plan and factor that amount into your overall withdrawal rate.

- **The unpredictable:** Basically, give yourself some financial wiggle room. Savvy income planning attempts to allow for factors you can't predict—and that aren't within your control. These include, for example, market volatility, your portfolio's performance relative to the overall market, inflation, and a change in personal circumstances. Build a cushion into your plan to help you weather these events.

Tips for Taking Early Retirement

For many of us, early retirement is the Holy Grail of all the hard work and retirement planning we've done throughout our lives. In a recent survey of workers ages 30 to 50, more than half plan to retire at age 60 or younger, and only 6% plan to work past age 65. Yet even if the balances of your retirement accounts have reached a level that satisfies you, you're not out of the woods yet, because tax penalties for taking distributions from those accounts before the official retirement age of 59½ can drain the accounts quickly.

In this section, we'll talk about ways you can take an early retirement while avoiding some of the tax implications. Let's start out with a case study about Clair Williams, a client of mine who went about early retirement in the wrong way!

How and When to Take Retirement Savings Distributions

- Make sure you understand the IRS rules for taking money from your tax-deferred accounts. There are penalties for both taking money too soon and too late.
- When retiring before age 59½, attempt to have a strategy in place for pulling money from tax-deferred accounts to avoid the early withdraw penalties.
- SEP IRAs, SIMPLE IRAs, traditional IRAs, and Roth IRAs all have similar names, but their rules differ. Get advice from a qualified adviser if you aren't certain which plan you have and which rules apply.
- Pay attention to the deadlines when you are the beneficiary of an IRA or qualified plan. The choices you make could have huge tax implications if the deadlines aren't met.

CASE STUDY

Clair Williams, technology executive

Clair had always dreamed of taking early retirement, and at the end of 1999, she felt it was finally within her grasp. After working for a technology company for 10 years and investing aggressively, she had accumulated more than $1 million in her company's 401(k). Clair worked for Lucent, and the company stock had been doing extremely well ever since it was spun off from AT&T.

Clair was 55 years old. Her pension would be small because she hadn't worked for Lucent very long, and there would be a penalty for retiring before age 59½. However, she calculated her 401(k) account had averaged more than 20% per year. Clair knew she couldn't count on those high returns every year, but she thought just drawing 10% per year would provide over $100,000 a year.

Unfortunately the stock market peaked in early 2000—just two months after Clair retired. Technology companies like Lucent were hit especially hard. Clair had left her money in the company 401(k) because she could take distributions without an IRS penalty after age 55. She cut back on her distributions when the market started to decline, but she didn't cut back on her position in Lucent, because the company had been hit hard a couple of times in the past but had always bounced back. Clair felt if she could just ride it out, the stock would bounce back, and she'd be in good shape again. By the time she came to see me in the middle of 2001, her 401(k) had shrunk to $400,000.

3 Steps to Start Your Early Retirement Planning

Retirement at the typical retirement ages of 62 or 65 is complex enough and requires good long-term planning. Taking early retirement—and for purposes of this section, we'll define this as any age under 59½— has twice the complexity. Dealing with tax penalties from retirement accounts; adding another 10 or more years to your life expectancy; and the health insurance issue are just some of the complexities that make early retirement extremely challenging. Yet by starting early and following the steps in this book, you may be able to achieve that goal and enjoy a comfortable lifestyle. You can begin with these three steps.

STEP 1: START PREPARING EARLY

The sooner you retire, the less time you have to save. In addition, you'll need to withdraw money from your accounts sooner, which means it will need to last longer. Assume you won't be saving anything after retirement, due to having no earned income.

Your strategy should be to save as much as you can as early as you can while you're still working. The New Three-Legged Stool approach is still the right model even for early retirement, so you want to be accumulating in all three types of savings. The more you contribute now, the more your money may compound and grow for the time you need it. And the more it grows, the longer it may last.

Step 2: Determine How Much You Plan to Spend

Think about the type of life you want to lead after you stop working, then figure out how much your present lifestyle costs you and compare the two. You'll probably find some things will cost less in retirement while others will cost more. For example, will you be playing more golf? Traveling more?

RICK'S TIP: If you're serious about early retirement, you should cut your monthly expenses as much as possible, enabling you to put away every dollar you can.

Another significant consideration will be your long-term healthcare costs. Medicare benefits generally don't begin until age 65, and it's not a good idea to go without health coverage until age 65 if you retire early: A serious illness or injury could potentially wipe out your life savings. If you need to obtain private medical insurance before age 65, start by checking with your employer to find out if health coverage for retired employees is available. (See the "Affordable Care Act (ACA) and Early Retirement" section later in the chapter for insurance options before reaching age 65.)

You'll also need to factor in the effect of inflation on your retirement expenses. A 3½% inflation rate will double your expenses in 20 years. What you budget to maintain your lifestyle at age 55 will cost twice that at age 75 and will be three times as much at age 87.

RICK'S TIP: The financial press often reports one should estimate retirement expenses to be about 80% of those incurred before retirement. My experience has shown most people want to keep the same standard of living and just replace work-related expenses with the other expenses I mentioned earlier.

STEP 3: DETERMINE HOW MUCH YOU NEED TO ACCUMULATE IN SAVINGS

In general, you'll need enough money to take a 4% withdrawal and meet your budgeted expenses. For example, if your budget calls for spending $100,000 per year, you'll need to accumulate $2½ million in savings (4% of $2½ million is $100,000). This assumes no other sources of income, which is very likely when you retire before age 59½. Some companies that offer pensions will allow early retirees to access their pension at a discount.

Once you reach age 62, you'll be eligible to start drawing your Social Security benefits (unless Congress changes the rules again). You can use your expected benefits to reduce your monthly withdrawals when calculating the amount of savings you need. Going back to the earlier example of $100,000 as the goal for expenses, let's assume Social Security will pay $20,000 per year at age 62. You expect your investments to support the balance of $80,000, so you'll need to accumulate $2 million in savings to support those distributions.

Be aware the benefit estimate you receive from Social Security assumes you intend to work up to the point you start drawing and your earned income will be the same. Retiring earlier than 62 could alter those figures. It's important to read the "Understanding Social Security" section to determine the impact early retirement will have on your estimated benefits.

3 Methods for Avoiding the Premature-Withdrawal Penalty

After you've done all the number crunching and determined you can afford to retire early, where will the money come from? The strategy for using the New Three-Legged Stool is the same. However, there are some very important penalty situations to work around until you reach age 59½.

You may think early retirement is a wonderful thing. However, the IRS doesn't agree. As I mentioned earlier, the U.S. tax code generally deems age 59½ to be the earliest anyone should retire. You could face ugly tax bills when accessing tax-deferred retirement accounts. You'll almost certainly pay federal income tax, and you may even be subject to state income taxes in states that don't normally tax retirement income. Most importantly, there's a 10% premature-withdrawal penalty that needs to be addressed. It's not always possible to get around this penalty, but by planning your strategy around the following three methods, you can often avoid it.

1. ROTH IRA WITHDRAWALS

You know from reading the section on Roth IRAs that these accounts allow you to withdraw the money you contributed without penalty. Because all contributions to a Roth are made with after-tax dollars, there are no federal income taxes on the withdrawals as they are considered a return of your principal. The trick is in making sure you are only withdrawing contributions. Remember that the money in your Roth can potentially come from three different sources: your annual after-tax contributions; conversions of traditional IRAs to Roth IRAs; and the investment earnings on either your contributions or conversions.

Roth IRA distributions are considered to come from these three sources in the order listed above. The tax rules to withdrawals from these sources are as follows:

- **Annual Contributions:** You can withdraw contributions income-tax-free and penalty-free at any time. For the early retiree, this is a readily accessible source of cash.
- **Conversions:** You can't touch this money within five years of the date of conversion without incurring the 10% premature-withdrawal penalty. The tax was already paid on the principal, but you avoided the premature withdrawal penalty when you transferred the money directly from the IRA to the Roth. Conversion money is only a good source of cash if the funds have been in the Roth for at least five years.
- **Earnings:** Withdrawals before age 59½ will be subject to federal income taxes and even state income taxes in some states. You'll also be assessed the 10% premature-withdrawal penalty tax, unless you qualify for an IRA penalty exception described in Leg Two (see Chapter 2) under tax-deferred accounts. You should only draw earnings from your Roth IRA as a last resort.

2. COMPANY PLANS/401(K)S

The standard 10% premature-withdrawal penalty applies to IRAs for those younger than age 59½. But the penalty is waived for withdrawals from company plans and 401(k)s once you reach age 55. This is an important planning consideration for an early retiree. You need to check with your employer to determine what they'll allow you to do with these funds after you retire. Many employers won't permit periodic distributions, because in that case, the employer would continue to be responsible for reporting distributions and balances to the IRS. It's generally to their advantage to get you to take your funds and move on. Consider the following case study about my client Audrey Kaufman:

CASE STUDY

Audrey Kauffman, corporate executive

Audrey Kauffman wanted to retire at age 56 so she could be available to help care for her elderly mother. After reviewing her financial needs and running projections, we determined Audrey would need a total of $140,000 for the next three and a half years to supplement her pension and annuity payments. This put her in the early-retirement ballpark, though she faced a major obstacle: Nearly all of her savings were in the company 401(k) account.

Audrey had already put all of her after-tax savings toward a college education for her two sons. She was eligible to begin drawing the company pension immediately, and she had a non-qualified tax-deferred annuity we were able to annuitize that would supplement her income. Still, these sources combined would only provide about half of the income she'd need to get her to age 59½.

We checked with her employer's policies on distributions from the 401(k) plan for retirees and found Audrey only had two options: She could leave it in the plan untouched until she reached age 70½, or she had to take it all out at once. We could roll over the entire 401(k) to an IRA and start taking 72(t) distributions, which would avoid the penalty. The problem with this strategy was she'd be locked into it for five years, and she only needed to bridge 3½ years to get to age 59½.

Looking closer at the plan, we discovered Audrey had $25,000 in after-tax contributions in her 401(k). Those funds would be separated from the rest and paid to her without tax or penalty when the 401(k) was rolled over. We also found she had $75,000 in company stock that had a low cost basis, which made it attractive for the NUA strategy I described in Leg One (see Chapter 1).

Based on all of this information, Audrey decided to take the following steps:

- Do a full distribution of the 401(k) for 100% of the cash and none of the company stock.
- The distribution was to be split, with $50,000 going to Audrey and the balance going to her IRA.
- The company stock was distributed to her directly in-kind.

The full distribution of the 401(k) generated four checks: $25,000 to Audrey for the after-tax contributions; $50,000 to Audrey with 20% withheld for taxes (net to Audrey = $40,000); $10,000 to the IRS for the tax withholding; and a check for the balance made payable to her IRA custodian. She received a stock certificate for the company stock about two weeks later.

Upon completion, she had checks for $65,000 and a stock certificate worth $75,000. The transaction had an R/D Factor of 35 with no tax penalties. As long as she did a good job budgeting the funds, we projected they'd last her through age 59½, when she could begin taking distributions with no penalty.

---

3. 72(T) PAYMENTS

72(t) payments, which we talked about previously, are generally the surest way to make yourself eligible for penalty-free retirement account withdrawals before age 59½. To implement these payments in your early retirement strategy, simply follow these three basic rules:

1. You must take a series of withdrawals (at least annually) with the amounts based on one of three methods discussed in the last section: minimum distribution, fixed amortization, or fixed annuitization.
2. With a company plan or 401(k), you must be separated from service. That means you must have quit, retired, been laid off or fired, or otherwise left your job. With a

traditional, Roth, SEP, or SIMPLE IRA, you can use the 72(t) strategy at any time.

3. Once you start taking 72(t) withdrawals, you must stick with the program for at least five years or until you reach age 59½, whichever comes *later*. You can't modify the account or payments in any way. To do so will subject all payments taken under the plan to the 10% premature withdrawal penalty.

The following case study about Sam Johnson demonstrates the value of using the 72(t) method.

CASE STUDY

Sam Johnson, early retiree

Sam Johnson took early retirement and set up 72(t) distributions from his IRA rollover account. His wife was 10 years younger and still working. She added Sam to her company's medical insurance plan and planned to cover him until he was eligible for Medicare. Three years later, Sam's wife was laid off from her job. She'd worked for a small employer that wasn't required to offer COBRA coverage. Sam was concerned that neither of them would have medical coverage. He called his former employer, who offered him his job back immediately with full benefits.

Sam no longer needed the 72(t) distributions, but he knew he was required to keep taking them. He decided to start putting money into the company 401(k) again to offset the income from his IRA. However, the next enrollment period wasn't until the following year. His accountant told him he was eligible to make a deductible IRA contribution, so he did. Unfortunately, he put it in the same IRA account from which he was taking 72(t) distributions. The three years of distributions now all became subject to the 10% premature withdrawal penalty.

What Sam didn't know is that he could have several IRA accounts and take 72(t) distributions from just one of them. My recommendation in this circumstance would have been to determine the amount of income the client wants, then calculate what the account balance needs to be to generate that amount. For example, a client age 55 wants $1,000 per month from his IRA. Using the fixed amortization method and the single life expectancy table, the client would need $198,575 in his IRA. For this type of client, I would recommend splitting his IRA into two separate IRAs: one holding $198,575 and the other containing the remaining balance. The 72(t) would be taken from the first IRA. If the client decides to make an IRA contribution later like Sam Johnson did, he can add it to the second IRA account without disturbing his 72(t) account. Should he decide $1,000 per month isn't enough, he could divide the second account again and start another 72(t) distribution.

Taking the chance of retiring early is a big risk. Early retirement requires a long-term savings and investing plan, and it takes discipline. This means keeping debt down and perhaps not living as lavishly now, so you can reap the benefits later. If you start planning early in life and do your homework, early retirement may be for you.

Finally—and this is critical—seek a competent, experienced financial planner to double-check your numbers. As you'll learn more about in the next section, this planner can serve as a sounding board to give you a second opinion about your retirement strategy and investment allocations. After all, you'll hopefully only plan for retirement once, so you need to do it right! An experienced planner has probably helped hundreds of people retire and knows what to look for or when something might be out of place. An experienced planner would have, for example, advised Clair Williams (from earlier in the chapter) to keep working, because a 10% withdrawal rate was too high. Had she kept her job, she would've been able to ride out the stock market drop and would probably be retired today. Instead, she'll be working at least part-time well into her 70s.

RICK'S TIP: If you go through all the recommended steps and determine you can retire early, do you know what you'll do with your time? I can tell you many stories of clients who retired in their 60s and were bored after a year. When you start making a financial plan to retire early, start planning what you're going to do with your time when that day comes. Make sure you have something to do and look forward to before you retire—at any age!

Affordable Care Act (ACA) and Early Retirement

One often-overlooked bright spot of the ACA is the opportunity it creates for those wishing to retire before age 65. People who can otherwise afford to retire before age 65 often remain at their jobs to keep their insurance coverage. Before the ACA, anyone with a pre-existing condition might not have been able to obtain private insurance. The ACA prohibits denying coverage for pre-existing conditions.

Now, those wishing to retire before reaching Medicare age can purchase insurance on the healthcare exchanges. Insurance companies can set premiums up to three times higher for those older than 50. However, the final cost of these policies may be held down by cost-sharing subsidies and refundable tax credits to cover the premiums. Qualifying for the tax credits is based on income, and proper income planning can help assure an early retiree that the premiums are affordable. In 2016, subsidies are available for single filers with annual income between $11,770 and $47,080, and for joint filers with income from $24,250 to $97,000 (family of four). Premiums cannot be more than 9.5% of income at the upper end of these ranges.

The income calculation to qualify for the subsidies is based on modified adjusted gross income, which includes wages, interest, dividends, capital gains, pensions, withdrawals from retirement plans, and, potentially, Social Security benefits. Many of these types

Early Retirement

- Use realistic rates of return for your projections and the safe withdrawal rates from the Trinity Study to determine if you have enough savings to retire.
- Early retirement requires disciplined savings and careful planning. Start early. You'll need to accumulate more money in a shorter period of time.
- Employers have a lot of flexibility in setting the rules for how their plans work. Make sure you know the rules for distributions from your employer's plan. You don't want to take an early retirement only to find out you can't get to the money in your company plan.
- The IRS doesn't like people taking early retirement. They've set up road blocks to keep you from getting to your retirement funds. Make sure you have adequate after-tax savings if you're planning to retire early so you can avoid unnecessary taxes and penalties.

of income can be controlled and minimized. The timing of drawing pension benefits, using growth oriented investments in taxable accounts, and sheltering earned income with retirement plans are all tools and techniques we can use to reduce taxes and now, insurance costs.

Taking early retirement requires careful planning because financial requirements are compounded by additional years of life expectancy. Your money needs to last even longer. The ACA may provide an opportunity to make early retirement a possibility by reducing the cost of one of the biggest expenses retirees face.

Get Guidance From a Good Financial Adviser

One of the biggest dangers people face when planning for retirement is knowing how to differentiate good financial advice from bad. The following case study about retirees Walter and Bernice Kimball demonstrates what can happen if you don't take the time to seek out the right advice before you retire.

CASE STUDY

Walter and Bernice Kimball, retirees

Walter and Bernice Kimball had dreamed of retiring at age 65 so they could travel and pursue their hobbies. They didn't get a lot of guidance from financial advisers throughout their lives, thinking instead being good savers was enough. They participated in their employers' 401(k) plans for their entire professional lives. The Kimballs also set a little money aside in after-tax accounts and, after Bernice received an inheritance of $250,000 in the 1990s, she put this money away for retirement, too.

The Kimballs sought advice from an adviser about how to invest Bernice's inheritance. The adviser sold them a variable annuity, explaining that the earnings would be tax-deferred and the principal was guaranteed. The Kimballs invested the entire inheritance amount in the annuity.

Had the adviser been following the New Three-Legged Stool strategy for retirement, he would've seen the Kimballs were already overweighted in tax-deferred accounts. They should have invested the inheritance after-tax and used the earnings to fund Roth IRAs for both of them each year.

Finally, the Kimballs turned 65 and had accumulated $1 million in their various retirement accounts, a savings they felt made them ready to retire and enjoy the fruits of their hard work. Yet because the majority of this savings was in their tax-deferred 401(k) plans, the Kimballs' overall retirement picture was not quite as rosy as it appeared.

Unfortunately, Walter and Bernice soon learned $1 million before taxes isn't the same as $1 million after taxes. Their retirement spending plan required an after-tax cash flow of $5,000 per month. Social Security would provide $2,500 per month, so the balance needed to come from investments. They had $100,000 in joint savings, $300,000 in the non-qualified variable annuity, and $600,000 in the 401(k) plans that had been rolled over to IRA accounts.

They decided not to touch the joint savings, so it would be available for emergencies or for large purchases they may need to make in the future. The $2,500 would come from either the annuity or IRAs, but either way, it would be taxable as ordinary income.

To complicate matters, taking $30,000 of ordinary income makes part of their Social Security taxable resulting in a tax bill of about $2,000. Walter and Bernice would be in the ugly tax bracket where part of their Social Security would be taxed. Increasing their annual income by $1,000 would actually increase taxable income by $1,500 or more.

The Kimballs' IRA funds could be withdrawn in a lump sum in one year, exposing 85% of their Social Security to tax in just one year instead of spreading it out over several years. However, they'd pay a higher tax rate on most of the withdrawal. The money would be invested in an after-tax account, generating taxable income that could make their Social Security benefits taxable anyway.

Clearly, the Kimballs needed help rethinking their retirement savings plan before they could reach their goals. They finally sought out a good financial adviser who redirected their plan in a much more tax-efficient direction.

The adviser recommended the couple capitalize on the better option of annuitizing their variable annuity. Annuitization is the process of taking an asset and, by way of an installment sale or annuity sale, effectively converting the asset into a stream of payments. Bernice would surrender her policy to the insurance company in exchange for a stream of payments called a payout option.

Bernice chose to annuitize her contract over 10 years, during which she'd receive 120 payments of $2,900 each; $806 of each payment would be considered interest and taxed as ordinary income, and $2,094 of each payment would be considered a return of principal and wouldn't be taxed or used in the calculation to determine the taxability of her Social Security. If she were to die before the 10 years were completed, the payments would continue to her designated beneficiary.

This change made Walter and Bernice's income tax projection completely different. Less than $10,000 per year of the annuity payment became taxable, so none of their Social Security benefits would be subject to tax. The standard deduction and personal exemptions would shelter the annuity income, resulting in a zero tax liability.

Fortunately, the Kimballs' new adviser wasn't short-sighted enough to stop the strategy there, because the annuity payments would end in 10 years, and the couple would simply be faced with the same problem all over again. In five years, both Walter and Bernice would turn 70½ and would be required to start taking withdrawals from their IRAs to meet the required minimum distribution (RMD). They would need to take advantage of the tax situation they created and continue to pull money from the tax-deferred accounts.

> **RICK'S TIP:** Some payout options guarantee income for as long as you live; other options spread your distribution out over the number of years you choose. Guaranteed lifetime options include life income only, life income with a guaranteed number of payments, and joint life payments. Non-lifetime options include payments for a fixed number of years or payments of a specified amount. You choose the form of distribution when you're ready to begin receiving payments, and the decision is irrevocable.

Each year, the couple decided to convert $17,000 of their IRAs to Roth IRAs. Converting this amount would make $3,800 of their Social Security benefits subject to tax. After claiming the standard deduction and personal exemptions, their taxable income would only be $13,000 and would be taxed at the 10% rate. Therefore, their strategy for the next five years was changed to convert the maximum amount from their rollover IRAs to Roth IRAs and stay in the 10% tax bracket. Their rollover IRAs would still likely grow, even with the conversions. At 6% per year, the IRAs would grow to $700,000, and their first year RMD would be $25,600. (Note: RMDs aren't eligible for conversion to Roth IRAs.) The Roth IRAs would potentially grow to $100,000 in the same period of time.

Walter and Bernice accomplished several important objectives at the end of their five-year strategy. First, they produced their monthly income goal of $5,000 in a very tax-efficient manner. Second, the Roth conversions slowed the growth of their rollover IRAs so their RMD became $25,600. This figure is $3,600 less than it would've been without the Roth conversions. Lastly, they built up a $100,000 tax-free source of funds. Should they need a lump sum of money to buy a car or take an extravagant vacation, they could now choose to withdraw from the joint savings or the Roth, depending on the tax implications.

This complicated problem was dealt with after the Kimballs were ready to retire. Had they hired a good financial adviser to help them map out a solid plan long before retirement, they could have avoided the whole mess.

"Great idea," you're probably thinking, "but how on earth do I find a good adviser?" The answer to this question is compounded by the entry of new players in the business of advice drawn by the immense revenue opportunities available today.

Unless you understand the difference between advisers and planners, you'll likely be disappointed and lose faith in the entire industry. Beware many financial planners today are salespeople in advisers' clothing. This indictment includes some stockbrokers, insurance salesmen, and tax advisers who have changed their titles to "financial planner." Often these individuals desire to sell products. There's little regulation in this area, and many individuals who call themselves financial planners aren't licensed.

Studies confirm individuals managing their own money tend to lack discipline, and those working with financial planners, who are often commission brokers, aren't doing much better. That's because many individuals working with a financial planner or stockbroker are adding value only in one dimension. Though it's true a broker can help investors by providing some discipline, the tools brokers use are often inappropriate for developing an overall strategy.

It's critical for investors to find an adviser who understands asset class investing and utilizes this latest tool, previously available to only the largest pension plans. Often investors and inexperienced advisers believe once they build an asset class portfolio, they won't need to make any changes. Yet if we look back only five years, we can see asset class investing has improved dramatically. Over the next five years, it's likely we'll see even greater changes. It would be foolish for an investor not to take advantage of this enormous opportunity. Finding an adviser to help utilize asset class investing and stay abreast of any new improvements will add tremendous value to an investor's portfolio.

RICK'S TIP: Focus on Fiduciary (*www.napfa.org/consumer /FocusOnFiduciary.asp*) explains the differences between advisers and brokers. The Website provides questionnaires to use when interviewing advisers. There is also a "Find an adviser" tab to use when searching advisers in your area.

Find the Right Adviser

When you interview potential new advisers, bring along the following list of key questions—and expect the following answers:

- **What's your professional background? Certified Financial Planner™ (CFP)? Licenses? Training? Credentials? (Remember to verify all answers after the meeting.)** Preferred registrations and licenses include:
    - Certified Financial Planner® or Chartered Financial Counselor.
    - Personal Financial Specialist (PFS).
    - Registered Investment Adviser.
    - NAPFA Registered Investment Advisor.
    - MS Personal Financial Planning.
- **How long have you been in the community and in this business?** Both the CFP Board and NAPFA (the National Association of Personal Financial Advisors) require a minimum of at least three years of qualifying full-time work experience for certification.

- **Are you registered with the SEC and/or your state's Department of Corporations?** The adviser should be registered with one or both.
- **Can you provide references?** Ask for references to clients that have similar circumstances to your own situation—preferably clients who retired from the same company you work for currently. If the adviser has had clients who retired from your employer, he or she will be familiar with your company's retirement plan and benefits. Ask for new clients as well as clients that have been with the adviser for several years.
- **Will you be giving me a written contract?** The agreement should clearly spell out how the adviser will be compensated and give the conditions for which the agreement can be terminated. You should also be given a current copy of the firm's ADV part II. This form is like a prospectus on an advisory firm and explains potential conflicts of interest.
- **What tasks will you perform?** At a minimum, a financial adviser should:
    - Work with you to determine your time horizon for investing. No one should ever invest without at least a five-year time horizon. Even for retirees, a five-year or longer horizon fits most situations.
    - Remind you there will be down years, and help you maintain an investment position that permits you to ride through those years without losing sleep.

- Help you set target rates of return and structure the investment strategy in a way that the return of the entire investment portfolio can achieve your objectives with the least amount of risk.
- Write out a financial plan with you. (I go into more detail about written financial plans in the Appendix.) This plan should be very specific and cover topics such as: target rates of return, risk tolerance, anticipated withdrawals or contributions, and desired holding periods.
- Rebalance your plan periodically. If an asset class differs by more than 5% from its original target allocation, adjustments should be made until the target percentage is restored. The adviser should look frequently at your overall balance, especially when the financial markets are setting new highs.
- Provide some method of measurement and measure your investment performance quarterly. It should be determined, using time-weighted rates of return, whether the market value of the portfolio is growing fast enough to achieve your target objective.
- Highlight the advantages of lower volatility, high relative returns, and determine why a particular manager's performance is leading or lagging the market. These are key elements in identifying a trend and getting in front of it. This goes way beyond just identifying the managers who've had exceptionally good performance near-term.

- When making a mutual fund selection, or when contemplating the termination of a mutual fund, the adviser must look at how long a manager's performance has been lagging behind market averages and/or their peer group averages. Keep in mind the market average is a compilation of all the different stocks that fall into every one of the management disciplines. The certain segments which will be leading will actually be the ones that are influencing the averages.

- **How will you be paid? By whom?** Advisers should be compensated on a fee-only basis rather than by brokerage commissions. Advisers paid with commissions aren't held to a fiduciary standard. They are not required to put the client's interests first, nor do they have to disclose conflicts of interest. In contrast, a fee-only adviser has a more objective position and is more likely to follow one of the modern investment strategies.

We've covered a lot of ground about retirement plans, but there's one big topic we haven't yet tackled: Social Security. Pick up a newspaper on any given day, and you're likely to encounter at least one story about how this traditional retirement plan is in big trouble. In the next chapter, I'll help you understand the origins of this government-sponsored retirement approach and how to access your share in a tax-efficient way. In addition, we'll cover the problems Social Security faces today and how we can go about getting the system back on the right track.

CHAPTER 5

Understanding Social Security

Social Security: A History

Most people think of Social Security as just a retirement plan, but it was actually designed to function as insurance against the loss of income due to retirement, disability, and the loss of a wage earner (survivor benefits).

Today, about 98% of all workers are in jobs covered by Social Security. More than 59 million people—one-sixth of the population—receive monthly Social Security (SSI) benefits, according to the 2014 Social Security Administration's Performance and Accountability Report.

According to the Social Security Website, Social Security benefits already comprise about 5% of the nation's total economic output. So,

RICK'S TIP: In fiscal year 2015, the program took in $920 billion and disbursed $897 billion.[1] It's a huge program that has grown to become an essential part of modern life and has been modified to provide for widows, orphans, the disabled, and divorced spouses. It will only grow larger as more of the Baby Boomer generation retires and the government struggles to come up with a way to pay their promised benefits.

how did this enormously important program come to be? The Website estimates over half of the elderly in American had insufficient income during the Great Depression.[2] Many states enacted legislation to provide some form of old-age pension, but these programs proved to be inadequate, and by 1935, 18 states had no program whatsoever. On August 14th of that year, President Roosevelt signed the Social Security Act into law. The new act provided a nationwide retirement and social welfare program for the first time. This program was designed to pay retired workers age 65 or older a continuing income after retirement.

We can never insure one hundred percent of the population against one hundred percent of the hazards and vicissitudes of life, but we have tried to frame a law which will give some measure of protection to the average citizen and to his family against the loss of a job and against poverty-ridden old age.
    —President Roosevelt, upon signing the Social Security Act

The new act contained two major parts: Title 1, which supplemented the state welfare programs for the elderly; and Title 2, which is the program we know today as Social Security. Originally, benefits were paid only to the primary worker based on payroll tax contributions made during the worker's life. Payroll taxes began in 1937, and benefits started in 1940.

How the system works today: Throughout an employee's career, a portion of his or her wages is paid to Social Security in the form of payroll taxes (FICA). Employers contribute an equal amount. Self-employed individuals pay both the employee and employer portion. In return, contributors receive certain benefits that can provide income when needed, either at retirement or upon becoming disabled. Family members can receive benefits based on an employee's earnings record also. The amount of benefits received depends on several factors, which we'll talk about in the next section.

Understanding Social Security

Be vigilant in checking your Social Security Earnings statement to be sure it is accurate. The statement is your personal record of the earnings you paid Social Security taxes on during your working years. The statement also provides an estimate of the benefits you and your family may receive as a result of those earnings. The statement is important in several ways:

1. The benefit estimates play an important role in your financial planning. Social Security benefits combine with your investments, pensions, and retirement accounts to make up your retirement income.

2. It provides a method to ensure your earnings are correct on your record. Any mistakes should be reported and corrected promptly. The sooner you identify mistakes, the easier it'll be to get the Social Security system to correct them.

3. The information in your statement is a record of the protection you've earned under Social Security for your family members should you become disabled or die before you reach retirement age. A copy should be kept with your estate planning documents.

Social Security Benefit Statements

Previously, Social Security benefit statements were mailed out every year. This was stopped in 2011 in order to save $70 million in annual costs. Benefit statements were still available, but only online. To view a statement online, workers are required to create an account at *SocialSecurity.gov/myaccount/*. The site requires you to provide some personal information about yourself and then answer a few unique questions that will be used to confirm your identity the next time you log in. The site instructs you to create a username and password for the account. Once you have an account, you can view your Social Security statement online at any time.

Unfortunately, only 6% of all workers signed up at the site. The Social Security Administration began sending statements again in 2014. Benefits statements are now sent every five years, not annually, and only to workers who haven't signed up online. Workers will be sent statements at ages 25, 30, 35, 40, 45, 50, 55, and 60.

The benefit statement contains an estimate of monthly benefits at various claiming ages and for disability claims. More importantly, it displays the worker's history of income subject to Social Security tax. This is a record of all payroll taxes received from the worker. It is important to review your benefit statement to verify your tax payments are credited correctly. Budget cuts have led to sharp reductions in customer service. Nationwide, Social Security staff is down to 62,000, from a peak of 70,000 in the 1990s. If taxes aren't credited properly, your benefit will not be calculated correctly at retirement. You don't want to step up to the payment window at age 67 to find only half the money you paid in has been recorded. The burden of proof will be on you. Don't wait for Social Security to mail you a statement every five years. Sign up online and check your benefits annually.

How Your Benefits Are Calculated

There are three components to determining your Social Security benefit: eligibility, average earnings, and age. Let's look at each one in detail.

3 Factors in Social Security Benefits

1. ELIGIBILITY

To be eligible for benefits, a worker needs to be employed and subject to Social Security taxes for 40 quarters. Each quarter you work earns you one work credit. Eligibility is based on the number of work credits you have. You need 40 work credits to be eligible to receive retirement income benefits if you were born in 1929 or later. People born before 1929 need fewer than 40 credits; fewer work credits are also required to receive disability benefits based on your age. A fully insured status enables the worker to receive unrestricted retirement, disability, and survivor payments. You earn a maximum of four credits in one year by working and paying Social Security taxes. Credits are based on your total wages (and/or self-employment income) during the year. In 2016, you must earn $1,260 in covered earnings to get one work credit and $5,040 to get the maximum four credits for the year.

2. AVERAGE EARNINGS

Social Security must first compute a worker's benefit by adjusting all of the earnings over their working life to reflect the change in general wage levels. Indexing ensures the worker's benefit will reflect the rise in the standard of living that has occurred during their working lifetime. Social Security will use the highest 35 years of earnings going back to 1951 to compute the average indexed monthly earnings (AIME). Table 5-1 shows the national average wage indexing series.

Insured workers become eligible for retirement benefits when they reach age 62. If 2016 were the year of eligibility, Social Security would divide the national average wage index for 2014 ($46,481.52) by the national average wage index for each year prior to 2014 in which the worker had earnings, then multiply each such ratio by the worker's earnings. This would give the indexed earnings for each year prior to 2014. Wages earned in or after 2014 would be used at face

National Average Wage Indexing Series, 1951–2014					
Year	Index	Year	Index	Year	Index
1951	2,799.16	1976	9,226.48	2001	32,921.92
1952	2,973.32	1977	9,779.44	2002	33,252.09
1953	3,139.44	1978	10,556.03	2003	34,064.95
1954	3,155.64	1979	11,479.46	2004	35,648.55
1955	3,301.44	1980	12,513.46	2005	36,952.94
1956	3,532.36	1981	13,773.10	2006	38,651.41
1957	3,641.72	1982	14,531.34	2007	40,405.48
1958	3,673.80	1983	15,239.24	2008	41,334.97
1959	3,855.80	1984	16,135.07	2009	40,711.61
1960	4,007.12	1985	16,822.51	2010	41,673.83
1961	4,086.76	1986	17,321.82	2011	42,979.61
1962	4,291.40	1987	18,426.51	2012	44,321.67
1963	4,396.64	1988	19,334.04	2013	44,888.16
1964	4,576.32	1989	20,099.55	2014	46,481.52
1965	4,658.72	1990	21,027.98		
1966	4,938.36	1991	21,811.60		
1967	5,213.44	1992	22,935.42		
1968	5,571.76	1993	23,132.67		
1969	5,893.76	1994	23,753.53		
1970	6,186.24	1995	24,705.66		
1971	6,497.08	1996	25,913.90		
1972	7,133.80	1997	27,426.00		
1973	7,580.16	1998	28,861.44		
1974	8,030.76	1999	30,469.84		
1975	8,630.92	2000	32,154.82		

value. If a worker didn't have 35 years of earnings, a zero would be entered for those years to reach a total of 35.

Once AIME is determined, the primary insurance amount (PIA) is used to determine the benefit. PIA is the benefit a worker would receive if he or she elected to begin receiving retirement benefits at his or her normal retirement age. This benefit amount is neither reduced for early retirement nor increased for delayed retirement.

The PIA is the sum of three separate percentages of portions of AIME. The portions depend on the year in which a worker attains age 62. In 2016, the portions are the first $856, the amount between $856 and $5,157, and the amount over $5,157. These dollar amounts are the "bend points" of the 2016 PIA formula. The bend points in 2016 are as follows:

- 90% of the first $856 of his/her average indexed monthly earnings, plus
- 32% of his/her average indexed monthly earnings over $856 and through $5,157, plus
- 15% of his/her average indexed monthly earnings over $5,157.

The resulting benefit amount can be affected by the final component of calculation: age.

3. AGE

Be aware if you were born before 1938, you'll be eligible for full Social Security retirement benefits at age 65, but if you were born in 1938 or later, the age at which you're eligible for full retirement benefits will be different. That's because normal retirement age is gradually increasing to age 67. Table 5-2 shows the current benefit as a percentage of PIA that's payable at certain ages.

As you can see, you can begin receiving early retirement benefits at age 62. Depending on your retirement age, the benefit amount may be equal to, less than, or greater than the AIME. If you choose to retire early—at 62, for example—the amount is reduced by approximately 0.56% for each month before typical retirement age. However, receiving early retirement benefits can be advantageous: Although you'll receive a reduced benefit if you retire early, you'll receive benefits for a longer period than someone who retires at full retirement age.

Year of Birth	Normal Retirement Age (NRA)	Credit for Each Year of Delayed Retirement After NRA (percent)	Benefit, as a Percentage of Primary Insurance Amount (PIA), Payable at Ages 62–67 and Age 70 — Benefit, as a Percentage of PIA, Beginning at Age—						
			62	63	64	65	66	67	70
1924	65	3	80	86 2/3	93 1/3	100	103	106	115
1925-26	65	3 1/2	80	86 2/3	93 1/3	100	103 1/2	107	117 1/2
1927-28	65	4	80	86 2/3	93 1/3	100	104	108	120
1929-30	65	4 1/2	80	86 2/3	93 1/3	100	104 1/2	109	122 1/2
1931-32	65	5	80	86 2/3	93 1/3	100	105	110	125
1933-34	65	5 1/2	80	86 2/3	93 1/3	100	105 1/2	111	127 1/2
1935-36	65	6	80	86 2/3	93 1/3	100	106	112	130
1937	65	6 1/2	80	86 2/3	93 1/3	100	106 1/2	113	132 1/2
1938	65, 2 mo.	6 1/2	79 1/6	85 5/9	92 2/9	98 8/9	105 5/12	111 11/12	131 5/12
1939	65, 4 mo.	7	78 1/3	84 4/9	91 1/9	97 7/9	104 2/3	111 2/3	132 2/3
1940	65, 6 mo.	7	77 1/2	83 1/3	90	96 2/3	103 1/2	110 1/2	131 1/2

Year									
1941	65, 8 mo.	7 1/2	76 2/3	82 2/9	88 8/9	95 5/9	102 1/2	110	132 1/2
1942	65, 10 mo.	7 1/2	75 5/6	81 1/9	87 7/9	94 4/9	101 1/4	108 3/4	131 1/4
1943-54	66	8	75	80	86 2/3	93 1/3	100	108	132
1955	66, 2 mo.	8	74 1/6	79 1/6	85 5/9	92 2/9	98 8/9	106 2/3	130 2/3
1956	66, 4 mo.	8	73 1/3	78 1/3	84 4/9	91 1/9	97 7/9	105 1/3	129 1/3
1957	66, 6 mo.	8	72 1/2	77 1/2	83 1/3	90	96 2/3	104	128
1958	66, 8 mo.	8	71 2/3	76 2/3	82 2/9	88 8/9	95 5/9	102 2/3	126 2/3
1959	66, 10 mo.	8	70 5/6	75 5/6	81 1/9	87 7/9	94 4/9	101 1/3	125 1/3
1960 and later	67	8	70	75	80	86 2/3	93 1/3	100	124

Note: Persons born on January 1 of any year should refer to the previous year of birth.

RICK'S TIP: You can also choose to delay receiving retirement benefits past normal retirement age. If you delay retirement, the Social Security benefit you eventually receive will be higher. That's because you'll receive a delayed retirement credit for each month you delay receiving retirement benefits, up to age 70. The amount of this credit varies, depending on your year of birth. If you elect to delay receiving benefits beyond the normal retirement age, but prior to age 70, the benefits are increased by 8% a year up to 140% of the normal benefit.

Family Benefits

As I mentioned at the beginning of this section, family members are entitled to a portion of a worker's benefits, under the specific circumstances described here:

- When a worker reaches retirement age, their spouse may elect to receive the greater of one-half of the worker's benefit or his or her own benefit. It doesn't matter if the primary worker is still working and hasn't begun to draw benefits; the spouse may draw at his or her eligible age.
- A divorced spouse who was married for 10 years or more to an insured worker may draw under the same rules as a married spouse. This doesn't impact the benefits available to the insured worker. As a matter of fact, the insured worker could have several divorced spouses drawing upon his or her benefit, and could also be currently married to a spouse drawing benefits.
- The minor children and spouse caring for minor children of a retired worker may be eligible for benefits. Children of retired workers younger than 18 (or 19, if

not graduated from high school) can qualify to receive
an amount equal to one-half of the retiree's benefit.
The same is true for a spouse if he or she is caring for a
minor under age 16. The total payable to a family is limited by a family maximum benefit calculation.

- Finally, if an insured worker passes on, his or her family
is entitled to certain benefits. Children younger than 18
(or 19, if not graduated from high school) receive a benefit, as does a spouse caring for a minor child under age
16. The amount is subject to family maximums and is
dependent upon the worker's AIME. A surviving spouse
(or qualifying ex-spouse) may elect to draw a widow's
benefit at age 60, whether or not he or she was married
to the worker at his or her time of death.

When to Begin Taking Benefits

When should I start drawing my Social Security benefits? I'm asked this
question more often than any other by my clients who are retiring
before Social Security's normal retirement age. They all want to know
if they should begin receiving benefits early with a smaller monthly
amount, or wait for a larger monthly payment later that they may not
receive as long. In answering this question for yourself, you should
take the following factors into consideration.

A few possible reasons to consider **drawing Social Security benefits early:**

- The financial challenges facing Social Security in the
future (which I discuss in more detail) are well known.
Though it's unlikely changes to benefits would be made
to those who are already retired, it could happen—
especially to those who have done a good job of preparing for retirement and have adequate retirement income
from other sources. You may delay drawing benefits only

How Social Security Benefits are Calculated

- Eligibility to receive Social Security benefits requires that a worker has been employed and subject to Social Security taxes for at least 40 quarters. A maximum of four credits can be earned in one year, and credits are based on total wages (and/or self-employment income) during the year.
- The Social Security Administration computes benefits by indexing all of the worker's earnings over their working life against general wage levels.
- Those born before 1938 may begin receiving full Social Security benefits at age 65; for anyone born after that date, the age at which they may receive benefits is gradually increasing to 67.
- Family members may be eligible to receive a portion of a worker's benefit if the members meet certain conditions.

to find out the amount you were expecting to receive has been changed. In the meantime, you'll have been using your own savings to live on.

- Social Security is largely based on life expectancy. If your family health history suggests your retirement is likely to be shorter, then it may be wise to start drawing benefits when you can.
- Drawing Social Security early allows you to preserve your own savings longer. You'll need income from somewhere if you're retired at age 62. You can keep your own savings invested and growing longer by using your Social Security benefits to meet your living expenses.

Considerations for possibly drawing Social Security benefits later:

- Will you be continuing to work and have earned income between age 62 and normal retirement age? Social Security benefits are penalized if you make over a certain amount of income. It wouldn't be wise to draw reduced benefits only to have them penalized.
- The Social Security Administration states if you live to the average life expectancy for your age, you'll receive about the same amount in lifetime benefits no matter when you start drawing benefits. In general, then, if you come from a family with longer life expectancies, you could do better by delaying your benefits until normal retirement age.
- Your spouse may be eligible for a benefit based on your work record. If you die before your spouse, he or she may be eligible for a survivor benefit based on your work record. This is particularly important if you've earned much more than your spouse over your lifetime. In this case, you may want to delay starting your benefits in order to provide your spouse with a higher amount.

Buyer's Remorse on Your Benefits

No matter how much thought and research you put into when to begin drawing your Social Security benefits, there is always the possibility you'll have buyer's remorse after you start. Believe it or not, the Social Security Administration permits you to stop drawing your benefits and then restart them later at the higher current rate. You probably won't be surprised when I tell you there's a bit of a catch: This option is only good for the first year of benefits and you must repay all of the benefits you've received to that point. However, you won't owe any interest, and there will be no adjustment for inflation.

To accomplish this, you must file Social Security Form 521—Request for Withdrawal of Application. You can download the form at the Social Security Website (*www.ssa.gov*). The administration will

> **RICK'S TIP:** If you've already paid tax on your benefits during that first year, you may be able to recover the taxes. You'll need to pick up a copy of the IRS publication 915, which has instructions and worksheets that guide you through the process.

calculate the amount you've been paid and request a check from you. Once you've paid back the benefits, you can apply again later for benefits and start drawing at the higher rate.

Suspending Social Security Benefits

You may also decide to suspend your Social Security benefits. If you have been drawing benefits for more than 12 months you are not permitted to repay the benefits and restart later. However, suspending benefits would allow your credits to begin increasing again from the time you suspend until age 70. Your benefits would automatically restart when you turn 70.

The reasons some people may want to suspend their benefits are pretty clear. If you started drawing benefits in your early 60s and are now getting a check for $1,000 per month, you may be able to stop that benefit and restart later with a higher amount. A little math can help you determine how many years it would take to come out ahead. On the other hand, you obviously need to live long enough to come out ahead.

Good health and a strong family history of long life expectancies are important factors in considering this strategy. The last point to consider is possible changes to the Social Security system which may reduce your benefits in the future. It seems highly unlikely benefits would be changed for existing retirees but it's a possibility. We all know Social Security is on shaky financial footing.

Changes to Social Security Claiming Strategies

Do you remember the days of full employment back in the 1990s? The unemployment rate was so low that the government was worried about a shortage of workers. Seniors drawing Social Security benefits were limited in the amount of income they could earn without penalizing their benefits until they reached age 70. In 2000, Congress passed the Senior Citizens Freedom to Work Act in an attempt to address both problems. The act eliminated the earned income limitations for a person drawing Social Security once they reached full retirement age. A senior could choose to work and continue to draw benefits or they could use a new concept called "voluntary suspension" of benefits. This would allow the senior to stop their Social Security payments and begin earning delayed retirement credits until they resumed taking benefits.

The new law's voluntary suspension rules also created some unintended consequences in the form of Social Security claiming strategies. Among these were the various "claim now, claim more later" techniques and the "File-and-Suspend" and "File-and-Restrict" strategies used by couples to boost the amount of Social Security they receive together. These strategies make use of claiming a spousal benefit (couples have some choices when claiming benefits in that when you claim Social Security you can select either your own benefit based on your earnings or your spousal benefit which is generally up to 50% of your spouse's benefit).

The Social Security Administration funded research to look at the cost of these planning strategies.[3] Their research found that the File-and-Suspend and File-and-Restrict strategies could cost the system about $500 million per year if couples followed an optimal claiming strategy. The relatively small cost is because only a small percentage (27%) of current couples can benefit. Only couples where the higher-wage earner's earnings were far greater than that of the lower-wage earner benefited from the strategy. The use of the more expensive "claim now, claim more later" strategy costs the system another $9 billion per year. Therefore, the potential annual cost to Social Security for these strategies is $9.5 billion per year. The Obama Administration targeted these strategies for elimination, calling them an "aggressive" move used by high-income households to "manipulate" benefits. The Bipartisan Budget Act of 2015 effectively ended these strategies.

What changed?

- **Restricted applications.** Seniors can no longer file for spousal-benefits-only at full retirement age and allow their own retirement benefit to continue growing.
- **Suspension of benefits.** There will no longer be the option to retroactively unsuspend benefits and receive a lump sum payment for the benefits you would have received since suspension.
- Nobody else will be able to receive benefits based on your Social Security record while your benefits are suspended.

Seniors will still be allowed to suspend benefits at full retirement age. The original intent of the Senior Citizens Freedom to Work Act was to enable a person who has filed for benefits and later goes back to work or otherwise changes his mind to suspend the benefit and accumulate the 8% annual delayed credits to age 70.

The one-year window to withdraw your Social Security application and pay back benefits is also unaffected. Repaying the benefits allows the retirement credits to begin accruing retroactively to the original filing date. Once more than a year has passed, you can still suspend benefits if you haven't reached age 70. Your benefits will be reduced for your early claiming, but suspending them can increase future benefits. Anyone currently using the File and Suspend strategy is grandfathered under the old rules and is not impacted by the changes.

Closing these so called "loopholes" didn't fix the long-term sustainability problems of the Social Security system. The Bipartisan Budget Act of 2015 changes are only estimated to reduce the Social

Security deficit by about 0.02 percentage points. Hopefully Congress will build on this small step to make the bigger changes needed to make the system financially sustainable for generations to come.

The Tax on Your Benefits—And How to Reduce It

Originally, the benefits received by retired workers weren't taxed as income because, the government reasoned, the money had already been subject to income tax. Once the Social Security system started having solvency issues (I talk about these problems in more detail in the next section), major legislation was passed in 1984 that was designed to address its impending insolvency. The legislation stipulated the portion of Social Security contributions paid by the employer hadn't, in fact, been taxed, so this portion of the benefit began being taxed for retired workers with incomes in excess of $25,000 filing as single, or with combined incomes of more than $32,000 for those married filing jointly.

The portion of the benefits potentially subject to tax was 50%, because this was considered the employer's contribution. In 1994, the portion of benefits potentially subject to tax was increased to 85%.

3 Steps to Determining Your Social Security Taxation

You can follow these three steps to determine the amount of your own benefit that's subject to tax.

RICK'S TIP: Keep in mind the amount of taxes a worker pays into the Social Security system isn't deductible from his or her federal income tax return—unlike state and local income taxes, which are deductible.

When to Begin Taking Social Security Benefits

- You may want to consider drawing Social Security benefits early if you believe the financial challenges currently facing the system will adversely affect your benefits, if you're unsure about the length of your life expectancy, or if you'd like to preserve your personal retirement savings.
- You could consider drawing Social Security benefits later if you will be continuing to work and have earned income between age 62 and normal retirement age, if you come from a family with longer life expectancies, or if you believe your spouse may outlive you and you want to provide him or her with a higher amount of your benefit.
- If you start taking your Social Security benefit and later wish you hadn't, you can stop drawing benefits and then restart them later at the higher current rate—but it must be done in the first 12 months and you must repay all of the benefits you've received to that point.
- You can still change your mind after 12 months by suspending benefits. This would allow your credits to start building again from that point until age 70. Benefits will automatically resume at age 70.

1. Calculate Your Total Income

This includes nearly everything: interest and dividend income, including tax-free municipal bond income; taxable pensions; other investment income; wages; net income from rental properties; farm income; and IRA distributions. What you can exclude are interest income from U.S. savings bonds, excludable foreign-earned income, and tax-free distributions from a Roth IRA. Don't include your Social Security income at this point.

2. Calculate Your Allowable Deductions

The government does allow some deductions from your total income. The first items would be any allowable income losses: capital gains (up to $3,000), losses from rental properties, business losses, farm income losses (you'd actually include these losses as part of the first step, when you calculate your total income). The other allowable losses appear at the bottom of page one on IRS form 1040. On the 2015 form 1040, these are the items in lines 23 through 35 and include contributions to an IRA or SEP IRA, Health Savings Account deductions, tuition and fees, self-employed health insurance, and so forth.

3. Determine Your Filing Status and Corresponding Benefits Tax

Your next step should be to figure out which of the filing status categories you fit into. This will then clue you in about your corresponding tax. Refer to Table 5-3 to find both.

3 Strategies to Reduce the Tax on Your Benefits

Knowing how Social Security benefits are taxed helps when devising strategies to minimize the taxation of those benefits.

1. Changing Investment Income

Many people structure their investments to produce income in retirement, because they're no longer working and now rely on their investment income to meet daily living expenses. It makes sense, then, to attempt to maximize the yield on their investments to produce the highest income. Investments like certificates of deposit (CDs), government and/or corporate bonds, preferred stocks, and income mutual funds are often used as the investments of choice.

This approach may make investment sense, but it doesn't make tax sense when drawing Social Security benefits. All of the income

If you income plus half of your benefits exceeds...	...50% of your Social Security benefits will be taxed.	...85% of your Social Security benefits will be taxed.
$25,000 if single, head of household, or qualifying widow(er)	X	
$32,000 if married, filling jointly	X	
$34,000 if single, head of household or qualifying widow(er)		X
$44,000 if married, filing jointly		X

produced by these investment vehicles will be used to make more of your benefits taxable. Income from municipal bonds and tax-free mutual funds are used to determine the taxable amount of your benefit, even though the interest from these investments isn't taxable.

For example, if you had $500,000 invested in income producing investments with an overall yield of 5%, the investment portfolio would be producing $25,000 of income, which would be used in the calculation for taxing your benefits. If you were a single filer, you'd already be at the first base level of taxation.

Instead of investing all of the money in income investments, you could invest $200,000 in a 10-year income annuity yielding 5%. The income annuity would make 120 monthly payments totaling $25,000 per year for 10 years. The remaining $300,000 could be invested in a growth vehicle like a tax-managed growth mutual fund or a variable annuity. Either one of these investments would produce little or no taxable income. If the growth investment averaged 5% per year, it would be worth $500,000 at the end of 10 years. The income annuity would be depleted to zero during the same time. You'd have maintained your principal and income stream.

The really exciting result of this strategy would be what happens to the taxation of your Social Security benefits. The $25,000 you'd receive as income wouldn't all be taxed as income, because $20,000 per year would be considered a return of your principal. Only $5,000 would be taxed as income, and only $5,000 would be used to determine the taxability of your benefits. At the end of the 10 years, you could split up your growth investment and do the same thing for another period of time.

2. PLANNING IRA DISTRIBUTIONS

Again, after you reach age 70½, you must begin taking minimum distributions from your IRA account. Those distributions are considered income to be used in determining the taxability of your Social Security benefits.

Most people will use the Uniform Lifetime Table we discussed previously to determine their minimum IRA distribution. It's the most commonly used of three life-expectancy charts that help retirement account holders figure mandatory distributions. (The other tables are for beneficiaries of retirement funds and account holders who have much younger spouses.) If you have an IRA balance of $100,000 at the end of the year before your 70½ birthday, you will be required to withdraw $3,650 according to the Uniform

RICK'S TIP: A similar result could be recognized by investing in growth-oriented mutual funds and taking systematic withdrawals. Part of each withdrawal would be considered a return of principal, and the rest would be taxed as earnings. Note however, this would be riskier than using an immediate annuity, because mutual funds aren't guaranteed. The tax on the investment earnings would be lower, because once you'd held the fund for one year, the distributions would be considered long-term capital gains, which currently have a lower rate of tax than annuity income.

Lifetime Table. Each year, if you remove only the minimum amount, the withdrawals should increase as you get older and the account continues to grow. If your income falls near the base amounts, these minimum distributions could prove costly in terms of the taxation of your Social Security benefits.

In this case, a little advance planning could go a long way toward reducing the tax on your benefits. One good plan for combatting this taxation is to consider a Roth conversion of the type we talked about earlier in the book. You could avoid minimum distributions altogether by converting your IRA to a Roth IRA all in one year. This would result in a large tax bill the year of the conversion, but you may avoid a lot of additional tax on your benefits in future years.

Another plan is to accelerate withdrawals into a single year. Until you reach age 70½ and must take minimum distributions, you have a lot of flexibility with IRA distributions. If you need to take $1,000 per month from your IRA for retirement income, you may want to take the $12,000 you need for next year in December of this year. This would accelerate the taxable income into every other year, potentially leaving you with a year of very little tax on Social Security benefits.

3. QUALIFIED IRA CHARITABLE DISTRIBUTIONS

The Qualified IRA Charitable Distribution (QCD) was first enacted in 2006 and then extended several times on a year-to-year basis. The Protecting Americans From Tax Hikes (PATH) Act of 2015 finally made the QCD a permanent part of the tax code. This provision allows individuals age 70½ and older to donate up to $100,000 from their IRA accounts to public charities without having to count the distribution as taxable income. The gift can only be made from traditional IRAs. Gifts from 403(b) plans, 401(k) plans, pensions, and other retirement plans do not qualify. Both spouses could gift $100,000 each on a joint tax return providing they both meet the requirements.

The ability to give directly to a charity from an IRA is a very important tax advantage for certain taxpayers. The provision allows

IRA owners who are 70½ to give directly to a charity and avoid reporting the income on their tax return. Taxpayers who take the standard deduction receive no benefit from charitable deductions, unless it comes out of their IRA. A QCD lowers modified adjusted income (MAGI), which could lower or eliminate the taxation of Social Security benefits.

The distribution must go directly from the IRA custodian to the charity to qualify as a QCD. The charity must acknowledge the gift for the taxpayer's records. The distribution is reported as a gross amount on line 15a of tax form 1040, but only the taxable amount carries over to line 15b. If the entire distribution went to the charity, then this number would be zero. "QCD" should be written next to line 15b to further identify the transaction.

Of course, these strategies require a lot of tax planning and projections. You should work with a skilled tax planner if you're uncomfortable running these projections on your own. There are a few additional shortcuts you can take to reduce the tax on your Social Security benefits:

- Make deductible IRA contributions if you have wages and are younger than 70½. If you have self-employment income, make SEP or SIMPLE contributions to reduce your income.
- Use tax-managed mutual funds or passively managed funds that are more tax efficient in your taxable accounts. Actively managed mutual funds that aren't specifically tax managed must distribute realized capital gains at the end of the year. The distributions are included as income in the calculation and could negate your efforts to minimize the tax on your benefits.
- Harvest unrealized losses at year end. Remember: You can take a maximum net loss from investments of $3,000 on your tax return. This loss can also be used in the benefit calculation to reduce income.

Reduce Taxes on Social Security Benefits

- To compute the taxes on your Social Security benefit, you must do the following three things: calculate your total income, calculate your allowable deductions, and determine your filing status.
- To reduce the tax, you can alter both your investment income and your IRA distributions in a tax-advantaged way.
- Charitably minded taxpayers with IRA required minimum distributions should consider QCDs to potentially lower tax on Social Security.

Social Security Reform

The Social Security system has been running surpluses since the 1980s, when we had the last major overhaul of the system. The surpluses are being accounted for in a trust that totaled $2.8 trillion at the end of 2015.[4] However, the first of 75 million Baby Boomers became eligible for early Social Security benefits at the beginning of 2008. As more people start drawing benefits, the system will cease to generate a surplus and will begin to draw on the trust fund assets. The following is the conclusion of the trustees from their 2015 report:

> Social Security's theoretical combined trust funds increase with the help of interest income through 2019 will allow full payment of scheduled benefits on a timely basis until the trust fund asset reserves become depleted in 2034. At that time, projected continuing income to the combined trust funds equals about 79% of program cost.... The Trustees recommend that lawmakers address the projected trust fund shortfalls in a timely way in order to phase in necessary changes gradually and give workers and beneficiaries time to adjust to them.[5]

Obviously, Social Security must be fixed. Because Social Security operates almost entirely as a pay-as-you-go system, it's been highly sensitive to the dramatic demographic changes over the last several decades. In addition to 8,000 Baby Boomers reaching retirement age each day, today's life expectancy of a healthy couple retiring at age 65 is 30 years.[6] The current system has only a little more than three workers to each retiree today, and that ratio will fall to two workers per retiree by 2030. Together, this falling ratio of workers to beneficiaries will push the system toward insolvency.

The sooner we act, the better. Every year we wait to address this problem, the cost of fixing it grows. The current system will soon start spending more money than it collects. Then it will begin using trust fund reserves, which are projected to be depleted in 2033. Once this happens, benefits will need to be cut 26%, or the government will need to come up with another $25 trillion to cover promised benefits through 2077. Though Social Security reform inevitably involves difficult choices, there's no future date at which those choices will be any less difficult than they are today.

Unrealistic Reform Options

It's clear Social Security can't continue to distribute future benefits at its current rate, but the question of what to do about it remains to be answered. Fix-It plans that have been proposed are:

Plan One: Immediately reduce benefits by 13%
Plan Two: Raise payroll taxes by 3.5% from the current 12.4%

It's pointless to compare the benefits or taxes related to the various reform proposals against benefit and tax levels of the current system, when the promises of the current system aren't fundable under existing scheduled tax rates. No matter which option the country chooses, there will be no free lunch: No one will get something for nothing. What we get out of Social Security is a function of what we put into it, so it follows that putting more taxes into the system will

> **RICK'S TIP:** Social Security taxes ought to be used for Social Security. Workers currently pay more into Social Security than is needed to pay current benefits. Because the federal government can't save this surplus, the so-called "trust fund" is really a deficit—a reflection of a liability, not an asset.

make workers worse off and retirees better off; putting less taxes into Social Security will do the opposite. We can't pretend these choices and trade-offs don't exist. Let's talk about those consequences as they relate to each option.

Consequences of Current Fix-It Plans

If Social Security benefits aren't immediately reduced by 13% (a very unpopular decision), then they'd have to be cut by 26% in 2033, growing to more than 32% in 2074. According to a recent study, these cuts would lead to a doubling of the poverty rate among seniors.[7]

Congress could also opt to increase taxes in order to maintain promised benefit levels. They could raise payroll taxes now from the current 12.4% to 15.9%[8] (again, a very unpopular decision). Failing to raise taxes now would require an eventual 50% increase in taxes by 2041, which would have a dramatic impact on our economy. Social Security is already the largest and most regressive federal tax paid by two-thirds of working families, 80% of whom already pay more in payroll taxes than they do in federal income taxes. It's a head tax on employment that's paid on the first dollar of wages earned, whether or not the company is profitable.

Another important consideration: When Social Security taxes go up in the United States, they don't go up in China. The trade implications of an increase in taxes would be immense. It's an underappreciated fact that increases in payroll taxes, particularly increases in the wage cap, will lead to dramatic reductions in employment.

Let's assume, then, we all agree that the current fix-it plans aren't viable options. Implementing one of them would result in either draconian benefit cuts, huge tax increases, or some combination of both. Yet obstruction and demagoguery of reform will, by default, result in the inevitable implementation of one of these plans.

Recent Proposals

CHAINED CPI

President Obama's 2014 budget proposal called for a reduction in future Social Security outlays by changing the annual cost-of-living increase to a method called chained CPI. The change is estimated to reduce the federal budget deficit by $340 billion over the next 10 years.

Social Security benefits are currently adjusted annually by the Consumer Price Index (CPI). In 1996, the Boskin Commission studied CPI and determined it over-estimated inflation by 1.1%. CPI is used to calculate cost-of-living adjustments for various government programs and to index portions of the tax code to ensure that these programs and tax provisions keep pace with inflation. Using a more accurate measure of inflation than CPI would help achieve this goal while curbing lost revenue from tax provision changes. Overcompensating recipients for the true cost of living increases may actually be contributing to inflation.

Chained CPI was created by the Federal Bureau of Labor Statistics. It assumes consumers change their buying habits when goods and services become more expensive. If a consumer spends $20 per month on tomatoes and the price of tomatoes suddenly doubles, it is unlikely that their cost of living will go up by $20. Instead, the consumer is likely to buy another vegetable that is less expensive. This is known as substitution bias and is not accounted for in the current calculation of CPI.

Chained CPI is considered a more accurate measure of inflation because it better takes into account consumer behavior. Estimates indicate using chained CPI since 2000 would have lowered benefit increases by between 0.25% and 0.3% annually. The new methodology would not reduce current Social Security benefits. It slows the annual increase over time. The President's proposal went nowhere.

Means Testing

Anyone who has done a good job saving for their retirement on their own should consider the chance that Social Security benefits will be means tested in the future. This is an important factor to consider when planning the start of Social Security benefits. Means testing of benefits already takes place in the form of taxation. It would not be a big stretch to propose only providing monthly benefits to retirees who have less than a certain amount of non-Social Security annual income. Means testing could take the form of even more increases in income taxes, a reduction in benefits, a surtax, or some other method.[9]

One proposal suggested would reduce Social Security benefits for individual retirees with more than $55,000 of non-Social Security income.[10] Their benefits would be reduced by about 1.8% for every $1,000 of income they have over the threshold. The threshold would be doubled for couples drawing Social Security. This proposal would affect 9% of current Social Security recipients. This type of means testing is similar to what is already happening to Medicare Part B premiums. The Medicare Modernization Act of 2003 required that high-income enrollees pay higher premiums starting in 2007. These premium "adjustments" are based on the retiree's adjusted gross income. Single retirees whose income exceeds $85,000, and couples whose income exceeds $170,000, are subject to higher premium amounts. Income thresholds used to determine Part B premium adjustments for 2016 through 2019 are frozen at the 2010 levels.

Monthly Medicare Part B Premiums for 2016

Means testing could also come in the form of an asset-based cap instead of income based. In 2013, President Obama proposed capping tax-advantaged savings across all accounts at $3 million. An excise tax could be levied against those with more than $3 million in retirement accounts. There was a 15% excise tax imposed on excess distributions from qualified retirement plans, tax-sheltered annuities, and IRAs back in the mid-1990s. A similar tax could be reinstated with the proceeds dedicated to the Social Security trust fund.

The decision to draw Social Security benefits is an important one to all retirees. Be careful to consider all the important issues before making this decision. A qualified retirement planner can help you evaluate all your options.

Realistic Reform Criteria

I feel a more realistic approach to fixing the Social Security system would be to make changes to the system based on the following three criteria:

1. **Protect the benefits of those already in or near retirement.** Most workers born prior to 1950 don't have enough time to prepare their finances to adjust for potential Social Security reforms.

2. **Place the burden of reform on higher wage workers while protecting middle and low income workers.** Every future retiree under any reform plan that indexes benefits based on prices will be guaranteed a benefit in real dollars that's at least equal to the benefits received by today's retirees. The concept of "progressive indexing" promises lower and middle income workers substantially more than current retirees—while giving the highest wage workers an amount equal to today's retirees. Considering the size of the shortfall we face, this seems fair.

For Joint Filers

If your 2014 modified AGI is		Your 2016 monthly Part B premium will be:	Your 2016 monthly Part D surcharge will be:
More than:	But not over:		
$170,000	$214,000	$170.50	$12.70
$214,000	$320,000	$243.60	$32.80
$320,000	$428,000	$316.70	$52.80
$428,000		$389.80	$72.90

For Single Filers

If your 2014 modified AGI is		Your 2016 monthly Part B premium will be:	Your 2016 monthly Part D surcharge will be:
More than:	But not over:		
$85,000	$107,000	$170.50	$12.70
$107,000	$160,000	$243.60	$32.80
$160,000	$214,000	$316.70	$52.80
$214,000	--	$389.80	$72.90

RICK'S TIP: Means testing of Social Security benefits, if enacted, is most likely to take the form of an income-based test. The government already has the means to track income and the current Medicare Part B premium test is likely to be the model. Those who implement the New Three-Legged Stool strategy will be able to use these techniques to minimize the impact of means testing on their benefits.

3. **Personal savings accounts ought to be a part of Social Security reform.** Prudence calls for directing surplus Social Security taxes into personal accounts that are owned by, managed by, and protected for the American workers. This would keep prevent the federal government from raiding the Social Security trust fund like it does now in order to report lower budget deficits. Opponents

---

Social Security Reform

- Neither of the two primary ideas for fixing Social Security that are currently on the federal government's table—reducing benefits or raising payroll taxes—are viable options for truly fixing the program.
- The key to real reform is privatizing Social Security by creating personal retirement accounts in which all workers could save a portion of their payroll taxes.
- Any reform plan chosen should aim to protect the benefits of those who are near retirement or already retired, and the burden of reform should fall to higher wage earners in order to protect middle and lower wage earners.

---

of privatization claim diverting $134 billion of surplus payroll taxes into personal retirement accounts is "robbing Social Security." Yet using those same resources to fund other government programs and replacing the funds with IOUs is "protecting Social Security." This doesn't make any sense.

Safe investments and years of compounding would provide workers with real ownership of their retirements, real choices, and peace of mind the current system doesn't offer. Moreover, many young people don't believe Social Security will be there when they're ready to retire. Privatization may help restore their faith in the system.

———

No discussion on the topic of tax efficient retirement planning would be complete without covering the massive healthcare bill passed in 2010. The Affordable Care Act was enacted to address the issue of affordable healthcare and reduce the ranks of the uninsured. There are some good parts of the legislation but it comes with a huge price tag. Chapter 6 addresses the law and explains how several of the components could affect your retirement assets.

CHAPTER 6

The Patient Protection and Affordable Care Act

The Patient Protection and Affordable Care Act (PPACA), com-monly called the Affordable Care Act (ACA) or "ObamaCare," was signed into law by President Barack Obama on March 23, 2010. The goal of the ACA is to ensure that all Americans have access to quality, affordable healthcare, and to create the transformation within the healthcare system necessary to contain costs. Whether the law will achieve this goal remains to be seen. However, from a retirement planning viewpoint, the ACA presents challenges and opportunities that need to be reviewed.

The cost of the ACA is financed through several new taxes and tax changes. A big issue of contention was the requirement for all Americans to have health insurance or be penalized. The Supreme Court reviewed this issue and ruled in 2012 that the penalty will stay. The government successfully argued this was a tax and that Congress has the ability to impose taxes. The Supreme Court agreed. The ACA has several new taxes. It is estimated the ACA will raise over $480 billion in new taxes as it is being phased in through 2022.

Insurance Marketplaces

The new public insurance marketplaces (formerly called exchanges) began offering health insurance in 2013. The insurance exchanges are a good opportunity for people older than 50 who are too young for Medicare and don't have access to a group insurance plan. Premiums are allowed to be set up to three times higher for persons older than 50. However, net premium costs could be significantly offset by tax credits. Tax credits are available if your income falls between 100 and 400% of the federally defined poverty guideline (FPL). Families have a maximum out-of-pocket premium expense of 9.5% of their annual income at the upper end of the qualifying income level. The projected FPL for 2016 would make tax credits available for individuals with income between $11,770 and $47,080, and families of four with income from $24,250 to $97,000. PPACA tax credits use modified adjusted gross income (MAGI) to determine qualification.

The new marketplaces offer four levels of plans: Bronze, Silver, Gold, and Platinum. The difference in plans is based on premium levels and out-of-pocket expenses. Platinum plans have higher premiums but cover 90% of costs. Bronze plans have the lowest premiums but will only cover 60% of the enrollee's costs.

For example, a 60-year-old individual (non-smoker) with MAGI in excess of $46,000 and no dependents could sign up for a Silver plan with an annual premium of $8,200. Because this person is

RICK'S TIP: Using the New Three-Legged Stool strategy can help control reportable income enabling you to qualify for larger credits. The final rules are still being determined in 2016. 2014 was the first year credits were available.

over the income threshold, he would not be eligible for tax credits. However, the same individual with MAGI of $40,000, would qualify for some tax credits which would reduce the net premium to $3,800.

This is a significant savings, which creates a planning opportunity for those younger than 65, or a couple in which one spouse is younger than 65 and isn't yet eligible for Medicare. MAGI includes wages, salary, foreign income, interest, dividends, capital gains, and Social Security benefits. Households close to the income levels qualifying for tax credits should pay close attention to year-end tax planning. Deferring salary and delaying capital gains or harvesting losses could mean the difference between meaningful tax credits or none. Year-end planning should include strategies to assure income is kept below the subsidy ceiling if applicable. To assist your planning, the Kaiser Family Foundation has a subsidy calculator tool (available at *http://kff.org/interactive/subsidy-calculator/*). This tool illustrates health insurance premiums and subsidies for people purchasing insurance on their own in federal health insurance exchanges. Some state exchanges offer their own calculators using insurance pricing for their markets.

Each state had the option of creating its own marketplace or participating in the marketplace set up by the federal government. ACA has established a Website (*HealthCare.gov*) to assist you if you're not sure where to go in your state. Those who don't have access to the Internet or prefer in-person assistance can contact one of the health centers around the country that has been awarded grants to hire and train "navigators."

Medicare Surtax

The Medicare surtax is a 3.8% tax on the lesser of net investment income or modified adjusted gross income (MAGI) in excess of $250,000 for married taxpayers filing jointly and $200,000 for single taxpayers. The tricky part of this tax is defining net investment income (NII). Keep in mind that MAGI is a taxpayer's income before his or her itemized deductions. Also note the surtax does not apply to net investment income under the threshold. Nor does it apply to earned income over the threshold. However, earned income over the threshold is subject to the separate 0.9% Medicare surtax. Only net investment income over the threshold will be subject to the new tax.

The definition of NII is found in proposed regulation Section 1.1411-4(a)(1). It separates NII into three categories:

1. Interest, dividends, annuities, royalties, rents, substitute interest payments, and substitute dividend payment.
2. Income from a trade or business described in Section 1.1411-5.
3. Net gain attributable to the disposition of property.

The first category is understandable. Tax-exempt municipal bond interest is excluded, along with distributions from a qualified retirement plan. The second category generally excludes distributions from an S corporation, partnership, or sole proprietorship if it is your ordinary course of trade or business. These distributions are only subject to the tax if the trade or business income is "passive" to the taxpayer. In other words, you must participate in the trade or business to be exempt from the tax.

The final category defines a disposition as a sale, exchange, transfer, conversion, cash settlement, cancellation, termination, lapse, expiration, or other disposition. Section 1031 transfers of like kind property are excluded. The sale of a principal residence is also excluded under Section 121 if the taxpayer claimed the property as his primary

RICK'S TIP: The new Medicare surtax can be complex to calculate. You should consult a tax professional familiar with the calculations if you think it affects your situation.

residence for two of the last five years. Capital losses can also be used to reduce other capital gains and $3,000 of other investment income.

9 Ways to Minimize the Medicare Surtax

To minimize the impact of the Medicare surtax, you need to develop a plan and implement it as soon as possible. The ACA is a permanent law, so developing a long-term strategy to reduce the tax is a prudent course of action.

1. Municipal Bonds

President Obama had proposed taxing the interest paid on state and local bonds issued after 2012. Fortunately this has not happened in any tax legislation passed to date. This is a good time to shake the dust off your tax-free investing books. If protecting income from taxation is a priority, a fresh look at the tax-free, municipal bond market may be your cup of tea. Municipal bond portfolios should be diversified by municipality and type—revenue and general obligation. Pay attention to unfunded pension liabilities and what the municipality is doing (if anything) to address its pension problems. Municipals make up only 10% of the U.S. bond market. It is also prudent to diversify outside of municipal bonds into corporate bonds and U.S. government agencies. The interest on corporate and government bonds is taxable, so they should be held in tax-deferred accounts when possible. Interest on municipal bonds is tax-free.

> **RICK'S TIP:** Municipal bond interest is not subject to the surtax. The surtax is based on MAGI, and municipal bond interest is not used in the calculation of MAGI. This could be a great time to switch from taxable bonds to municipal bonds even with interest rates at historic lows.

2. Tax-Loss Harvesting

Year-end tax planning generally includes reviewing currently held security positions trading below cost. To use the loss for tax purposes, the position must be sold, creating a realized loss. The technique of creating these losses for tax planning is called tax-loss harvesting.

A common mistake occurs when an investor sells a position to harvest the loss with the objective of buying back the same security. Tax laws require waiting 30 days before repurchasing the same security. Failing to wait 30 days triggers the wash-sale rule, which disallows the loss for tax purposes. If the investor sells the security, and the market rallies before the 30 days have passed, the investor can easily end up paying more to buy back the security than was saved in taxes.

Capital losses can be used to offset capital gains and reduce NII. If losses exceed gains, a taxpayer can take a $3,000 loss against other income and reduce MAGI. Any excess loss can be carried forward into future tax years. Tax-loss harvesting has the potential to create havoc with investment strategy. Always begin with your investment strategy in mind and harvest losses where an investment change could enhance your portfolio as well as your tax situation.

3. Maximize Use of Retirement Accounts

Making contributions to an employer-sponsored plan is a great way for high-income taxpayers to shelter income and reduce MAGI. Deferring income can save itemized deductions subject to the Pease limitations and also avoids the 0.9% surtax that applies only to wages and self-employment income. Contributions grow tax-deferred inside the account and will not be subject to the surtax when distributed. (The Pease limitation on itemized deductions, named after Ohio Congressman Donald Pease, who helped create it, reduces most itemized deductions by 3% of the amount by which AGI exceeds a specified threshold, up to a maximum reduction of 80% of itemized deductions.)

For 2016, the elective deferral (contribution) limit for employees who participate in 401(k), 403(b), most 457 plans and the federal government's Thrift Savings Plan increased to $18,000. The catch-up contribution limit for employees age 50 and older who participate in 401(k), 403(b), most 457 plans, and the federal government's Thrift Savings Plan is $6,000.

4. Fund Charitable Goals With Appreciated Assets

A strategy for managing capital gains involves the use of a donor advised fund (DAF) for taking gains and fulfilling a client's charitable goals. A DAF is a separate account operated by a section 501(c)(3) organization, which is called the sponsoring organization. This organization has been created for the purpose of managing charitable donations on behalf of an organization, family, or individual. A DAF provides an easy-to-establish, low-cost, flexible vehicle for charitable giving. In exchange, the donor enjoys a convenient, cost-effective, and tax-advantaged way to make charitable gifts through the DAF.

One of the overlooked advantages of using a DAF is the ability to manage your capital gains. An investment position with a long-term gain could be moved to the DAF before it is sold. The gain is not taxable in a DAF and the proceeds can be used to make future charitable contributions. You simply hold the sale proceeds in the DAF until you determine which charity will ultimately receive the proceeds. DAFs can be used for rebalancing or to remove positions that have reached full value. Investments with unrealized losses should be sold outright to harvest the loss.

RICK'S TIP: Appreciated assets transferred to the DAF qualify as a charitable contribution. The donor may receive a federal income tax deduction up to 30% of adjusted gross income (AGI) for appreciated securities. Unfortunately some of this deduction may be phased out if the taxpayer is subject to the Pease itemized deduction limitations.

5. Establish a Charitable Remainder Trust

What if you need the income from an appreciated asset and can't afford an outright gift to a DAF? This strategy calls for the use of a special kind of trust known as a charitable remainder trust (CRT). The donor sets up an irrevocable trust naming a charity (or charities) as the beneficiary. Appreciated assets are transferred to the trust qualifying as a completed gift. The CRT is required to make payments to the donor at least annually during the term of the trust. Any remaining principal is then distributed to one or more charities at the end of the trust's term. The IRS allows a partial charitable deduction of the amount contributed and the income is only partially taxable.

Funding the trust with appreciated assets avoids capital gains tax when the assets are sold. The proceeds can then be reinvested into income-producing assets providing greater diversity, less risk, and perhaps more income than the one originally donated. This CRT pays the donor a fixed percentage (5% at minimum) of the trust assets determined each year. The assets may go up or down in value, and the annual payout will fluctuate accordingly. The donor shares in the investment risks and rewards through the changes in the payout each year. The trust can be set up as a charitable remainder annuity trust (CRAT). A CRAT pays out a fixed percentage of the initial value of trust assets, so the annual distribution remains constant through the trust's life.

6. Switch to Tax-Efficient Investments

The most tax-efficient investment strategy is simple: Hold shares for as long as possible, thus deferring the taxes on your capital gains until you sell. An extremely tax-efficient portfolio would therefore be a selection of growth-oriented assets held for the long haul. Assets that grow (as opposed to income producing) are preferred, because they tend to pay little or no dividends. Your return would be mostly made up of long-term capital gains. Best of all, you'd get to decide when you pay the tax by choosing when to sell them.

Among growth-oriented assets, tax-efficient funds are preferable because they offer diversification. The most tax-efficient funds are index funds, exchange traded funds, and those funds with the mandate of operating tax efficiently. Tax-efficient investing requires active involvement beginning with looking for tax-efficient mutual funds as discussed previously. The portfolio should be monitored so losses are harvested to offset gains when appropriate. It's important to keep in mind that investing tax efficiently is a balancing act. The reality is there will always be trade-offs; your overarching goal should be to minimize taxes while still attempting to achieve superior investment returns. Some investors make the mistake of holding, even when it's not wise to do so, rather than selling if the sale produces a capital gain. Remember: The tax decision should never overrule the investment decision. Assessing the tax consequences of your investments at each stage—contribution, accumulation, and distribution—is the key to success in the world of tax-advantaged investing.

7. Roth Contributions

As discussed earlier, upper-income taxpayers may not be able to make a direct Roth contribution. There are income limits phasing out a taxpayer's ability to contribute. In 2016, single taxpayers and heads of household who are covered by a retirement plan at work begin to phase out contributions when modified adjusted gross income

(MAGI) is between $117,000 and $132,000; joint filers when MAGI is between $184,000 and $194,000.

Even if your income is above the threshold you can still get money into a Roth IRA in a roundabout way. There are no income limits for making a non-deductible IRA contribution. The limit on annual contributions in 2016 is $5,500. The catch-up provision for anyone age 50 or older increases the maximum to $6,500. Since 2010, there are no income limits for converting a traditional IRA to a Roth IRA. A high-income taxpayer simply makes a non-deductible contribution to an IRA and then converts it to a Roth IRA. This strategy of indirectly contributing funds into a Roth IRA may not be effective for taxpayers who already have substantial amounts invested in a traditional IRA because of the "pro rata rule." This rule requires a taxpayer to include all IRA assets when determining the taxes due on a Roth conversion. Though investing indirectly in a Roth IRA isn't appropriate for everyone, it can provide a viable option to those with higher incomes who are otherwise unable to contribute to a Roth.

8. Roth Conversions

The taxable distribution created by converting a traditional IRA to a Roth isn't considered NII but it still increases MAGI, which could subject other income into NII. However, Roth conversions shouldn't be ruled out. Long-term tax planning should take into consideration the benefits of Roth conversions today to lessen required minimum distributions in the future. Review the "Roth IRA Conversions: Better Than Any Tax Break" section in Chapter 3 to determine if Roth Conversions are right for your situation.

9. Hire a Financial Adviser

Advisory fees have always been a deductible expense for taxpayers who itemize. The IRS allows a tax deduction for certain investment-related expenses reported on Schedule A under miscellaneous itemized deductions subject to the 2%-of-AGI floor, and an AMT adjustment. The IRS has also determined the calculation to determine NII includes deductions properly allocable to earning gross investment income. Section 212 of the Internal Revenue Code details the deductibility of expenses associated with an individual's financial issues. There are three categories of deductible costs:

1. For the production or collection of income.
2. For the management, conservation, or maintenance of property held for the production of income.
3. In connection with the determination, collection, or refund of any tax.

Other ACA Taxes

There are four other taxes that began in 2013 that could affect you:

1. The medical itemized deduction was raised from 7.5% to 10% of adjusted gross income (AGI). This provision imposed a threshold of 10% of AGI before medical expenses are deductible. The raise is waived for seniors (age 65+) from 2013 to 2016.
2. Capping the popular Flexible Spending Account (FSA). The ACA imposes a cap of $2,550 in 2016 (indexed to

RICK'S TIP: Advisory fees can be used to reduce NII subject to the surtax and then deducted on Schedule A to reduce overall income taxes. Most importantly, a competent financial adviser will help you develop a strategy to minimize your total tax bill while helping you achieve your financial goals.

inflation annually) on FSAs. (There had been no limit.) Twenty-four million American taxpayers currently use their FSAs to purchase medical products and services. Thousands of families with special needs children use their FSAs to pay for special needs education, which can cost more than $10,000 per year per child. Under previous tax rules, FSA dollars could be used to pay for this type of special needs education.

3. 2.3% excise tax on medical device manufacturers. The new tax will be levied on the total revenues of a company, regardless of whether a company generates a profit. It has the potential to raise the price of everything from pacemakers to prosthetic limbs. There is an exemption for items retailing for less than $100.

4. Elimination of tax deduction for employer-provided retirement Rx drug coverage in coordination with Medicare Part D. How many employers do you think will continue to provide this benefit if it is no longer deductible?

Tax Penalty for the Uninsured

The ACA created a tax that started in 2014: the tax (or penalty if you prefer) on individuals without healthcare insurance. Taxpayers must have the minimum coverage as defined by the government for themselves and their dependents to avoid the tax. This requirement includes employer coverage, coverage purchased through an exchange, Medicare, Medicaid, and Tricare. The employer mandate requiring healthcare coverage for companies with 50 or more employees was delayed until 2016, but the individual mandate was not.

The tax in 2016 for being uninsured is the higher of:

- 2.5% of annual household income. (Only the amount of income above the tax filing threshold, about $10,000 for an individual, is used to calculate the penalty.) The maximum penalty is the national average premium for a Bronze plan.

- $695 per adult for the year ($347.50 per child under 18). The maximum penalty per family using this method is $2,085.

Both of these levels are set to increase in 2017. The tax cannot exceed what a Bronze-level plan would cost the taxpayer, if purchased on the healthcare exchange. The tax is reduced pro-rata for each month the taxpayer had healthcare coverage.

Taxpayers may qualify for an exemption from the tax if the premium cost of their share of employer provided insurance exceeds 8% of household AGI. Likewise, taxpayers are exempt if the cost of a basic Bronze-level plan on the exchange exceeds 8% of AGI. Exemptions are also available for members of religious groups opposed to private or public insurance and those who can show hardship.

RICK'S TIP: The IRS is responsible for monitoring compliance and levying the tax. Employers are mandatorily required to report details of employee coverage. The tax is collected annually on IRS form 1040.

Healthcare Costs and the New Three-Legged Stool

Probably one of the biggest concerns for people planning their retirement is having enough money. Directly related to this concern is the cost of healthcare. What will healthcare cost in retirement? Can I effectively manage the cost of healthcare? There's a lot that can be done to manage the cost of healthcare through proper planning. How funds are saved and invested will play an important role.

Medicare plays an important part in retirement healthcare costs. Medicare Part A, which is hospitalization, has already been paid for through FICA taxes while the retiree was working. Medicare Part B covers doctor visits, emergency room visits, tests, and things of that nature. Part B premiums are usually deducted from Social Security benefits. Medicare Part D covers prescription drugs. Part D premiums are also deducted from Social Security benefits. Finally there are supplemental policies, or Medigap insurance. Medicare doesn't cover everything. Estimates project only about half of someone's medical expenses are covered. Most retirees need to purchase additional insurance to actually cover the remaining costs through a Medigap policy.

Medicare Advantage is a combination of Medicare's Part A, B, and D and Medigap. The difference is that Medicare Advantage is primarily an HMO, where Medigap is primarily a PPO. The premiums are deducted from Social Security benefits but go to the Medicare Advantage provider instead of Medicare.

Healthcare costs for retirees have changed dramatically over the past 25 years, and more changes are coming. Most retirees didn't buy Medigap policies in the past because their employer provided that coverage as a retiree benefit. That perk is either going away completely or the cost shared by the retiree makes buying their own Medigap coverage more attractive. Fidelity has estimated the cost of supplement insurance and out-of-pocket prescription costs at $260,000–$270,000 during retirement.[1]

We should expect that as time goes on retirees will be more and more responsible for their own healthcare expenses. Deductibles for pre-retirement commercial insurance have increased by some 50% over the last 10 years. It's estimated that 20% of the working population is already in a high deductible plan.

In addition to these changes, healthcare costs are projected to inflate at 6–6.5% going forward.[2] This comes at a time retirees are expected to live even longer. The Society of Actuaries projects that life expectancy increases a little more than a month each year. A healthy 65-year-old couple planning for 25–30 years in retirement may actually have 30–35 years to live. What might that mean in additional healthcare costs?

Healthcare for Retirees

The government has chosen to address the increasing costs of Medicare through means testing. Upper-income retirees will pay higher premiums for Part B and D based on their income level. Income level is defined by Medicare as modified adjusted gross income (MAGI). Retirees will not be able to get around this by investing in tax-free bonds. Tax-free income is included in MAGI. Means testing currently affects singles with income in excess of $85,000 and couples with income of more than $170,000. These income levels are not indexed to inflation. The Center for Retirement Research at Boston College projects Part B premiums could jump from the standard monthly premium of $104.90 in 2016 to $510 for retirees in the top income bracket!

Retirees will need to pay close attention to means testing levels in order to contain healthcare costs. This requires careful planning before retirement. Strategies used in the New Three-Legged Stool to control income taxes will play an important role in controlling Medicare premiums. Retirees who save all of their money in a tax-deferred account will not only be forced to pay income taxes when they withdrawal their funds, they could also pay higher Medicare premiums.

The New Three-Legged Stool approach to retirement is based on balancing your savings among tax-deferred, after-tax, and tax-free accounts. Many people are not concerned with balancing their savings. They save money in the company 401(k) for retirement and spend everything else. When these people enter retirement they will have nothing but their tax-deferred savings to draw on. This will be coming at a time when the IRS could be even more aggressive in taxing these assets on top of means testing Medicare premiums.

John Sample has done a perfect job of saving for retirement and has completely balanced savings: $667,000 is in tax-deferred IRA/401(k) accounts, $667,000 is in an after-tax account, and $666,000 is in his Roth IRA tax-free account. His total retirement savings of $2 million can be expected to distribute 4% ($80,000) per year based on the prudent withdrawal rule. This income, if everything was in his 401(k) and IRA accounts and was all taxable, together with Social Security benefits of $25,000, would make his Medicare premiums subject to means testing.

However, because Mr. Sample saved tax efficiently the tax liability from the after-tax account is not necessarily based on the amount of withdrawal. And there is no tax liability from any qualified Roth withdrawals. Assuming Mr. Sample follows the asset location strategy we recommend, there will be some tax implications from dividend distributions and rebalancing. Mr. Sample will only need to report $47,000 of taxable income from the account withdrawal. Therefore, he will pay less in income taxes and his Medicare premium will not be subject to means testing.

The New Three-Legged Stool approach provides a retiree with the flexibility to pull the income needed from the most tax efficient location each year. This should become even more valuable as income taxes and Medicare premiums increase in the future.

―――――

By this point, we've covered nearly all of the bases involved in the game of retirement planning. There's just one more important topic I want to discuss: estate planning. Let's move on to Chapter 7, in which I review strategies to plan your estate in a manner that helps your heirs retain as much as possible.

CHAPTER 7

Curtail Effect the IRS Has on Your Estate

In a recent survey of affluent investors, 80% of respondents said they hadn't updated, reviewed, or had a conversation with regard to their estate plan in the last five years. What this likely means is that all of those respondents' estate plans have become outdated through circumstances such as changes in their family situations (marriage, new grandchildren, and so forth), net worth additions or subtractions, or business and/or partnership changes.

5 Reasons to Reexamine Your Estate Plan

There are many important reasons to periodically reexamine your estate plan and all of the documents related to it. These are my top five.

1. Your state has a plan for your estate. Everyone has an estate plan whether they know it or not: it's called "by default!" That is, if you die without a will, your state has backup laws in place that dictate the disposition of your assets after your death. This means that if you die without a will, the state decides who receives your assets—and there's no guarantee that the state will make the same decisions that you would have made.

    If you don't have an updated will, don't feel badly about it, because you're not alone. According to a recent survey, 60% of Americans believe adults should have a will, yet only 44% have one.[1] What's more, those who have a will often forget to update it.

2. You can safeguard your estate even if you become incapacitated. Should you become unable to make financial decisions, an estate plan allows you to designate someone to act on your behalf regarding your assets. You can also designate someone to be your surrogate to make decisions regarding your health and well-being.

3. Estate planning helps with difficult end-of-life decisions. Putting your wishes in writing relieves your family of the burden of making end-of-life decisions—decisions that may have profound emotional and financial consequences for them.

4. Estate planning minimizes taxes. You can maximize the amount of your estate that goes to heirs and minimize the amount that goes to the IRS.

5. You can support your favorite charities. If you have a favorite charity or cause, a gift from your estate can be an easy way to make a significant financial contribution.

Reexamine Your Estate Plan

- Keep your estate plan up-to-date. This ensures the disposition of your assets at death follows your wishes and not the rules of your state.
- Estate planning can minimize taxes and may maximize the amount that goes to your heirs.
- An estate plan and healthcare directive help your family carry out your wishes while minimizing conflict.
- Review your beneficiary designations on retirement plans and insurance policies to verify they are consistent with your estate plan.

Estate Tax Overview

When it comes to your estate, there are two main types of tax to consider: the federal estate tax and the federal gift tax. I summarize both in this section.

Federal Estate Tax

The American Taxpayer Relief Act of 2012 (ATRA12) finally brought some permanence to what has been a "patch and postpone" estate tax policy. Estate tax in the United States has been one important area of financial planning that needed a level of permanence. No longer will your estate planning be significantly impacted by what year you die. The exclusion amount is permanent and will be indexed to inflation each year, and the rate over the exclusion is fixed.

ATRA12 increased the tax rate on a taxable estate to 40%. The rate is up from the 35% it had been through 2012, but still less than the 45% rate proposed by President Obama. A change in the rate is the easiest change to deal with because it does not require the revision of familiar estate-planning techniques.

State inheritance and estate taxes are deductible in calculating the federal taxable estate. States that have their own estate tax coupled to the federal tax use the pre-2002 federal credit, with a top rate of 16% for taxable estates in excess of $10.1 million.

The estate tax exemption is $5.45 million per person in 2016 and is indexed for inflation each year. Essentially this means there is no federal estate tax owed until the value of your estate exceeds this amount. An important aspect of ATRA12 was the decision to make the portability rules for a deceased spouse's unused estate tax exemption amount permanent. This reduced the need to use a bypass trust for all but the wealthiest of families. This new "portability" of the unused exemption means a couple could exclude the first $10,900,000 of their estate without the need for a bypass trust. In order to claim portability, estates must file a timely estate tax return (even if not otherwise obligated to do so) and report the amount of the unused exemption that remains from the decedent as a carryover to the surviving spouse.

The step-up in cost basis for appreciated assets was retained in ATRA12. The effect of the increase in capital gains tax should be considered when deciding to make gifts of appreciated assets. There is no step-up in basis for assets gifted during lifetime. Assets transferred by gift retain the donor's basis except if the asset value on the date of gift is less than the donor's cost. A little-known rule gives the beneficiary a split basis, which prevents the donor from realizing the loss on the sale of the asset.

Federal Gift Tax

One of the most common ways retirees attempt to skirt estate taxes is to give portions of their estates away as gifts before they die (I explain more details about gifting strategies later in the chapter). But this approach isn't without its own tax rules, otherwise known as the federal gift tax. This tax is paid by the donor on gifts that exceed $14,000 to any one recipient annually. You can use your lifetime exclusion to shelter gifts up to $5.45 million. Basically, we all have a lifetime exclusion from estate taxes we can use while we're living to shelter gifts or upon our death to shelter our estate. However, when you're making gifts in excess of $14,000 annually to one person, you're using up your lifetime exclusion, which could mean your estate will pay a lot more taxes when it's settled.

The gift tax and estate tax are similar and are taxed on the same scale, with one important difference: The gift tax is pre-tax, and the estate tax is after tax. You don't include the gift taxes when figuring the value of a gift. The funds used to pay estate taxes are themselves subject to the tax. Therefore, a taxable gift is more favorable than having an asset taxed at death, because the funds used to pay gift taxes escape taxation.

Titling Assets Property

How you take title of assets can impact your estate, taxes, and perhaps the disposition of the asset if a couple divorces. Many couples want assets to be titled simply in the event something happens to one so the other can take possession immediately without taxes or

---

Understanding Estate Taxes

- The two main types of estate taxes are the federal estate tax and the federal gift tax.
- A portion of your estate may be excluded from the federal estate tax, but the amount of the exclusion varies from year to year.
- You can shield part of your estate from taxes by giving it away before you die, but the maximum amount you can give tax-free is $14,000 per person, per year, or $5.45 million total over your lifetime.

---

complications. Joint ownership may be the simplest way to meet most of these objectives. However, joint ownership can get messy in the event of any number of occurrences, such as divorce, second marriage, children from multiple marriages, adoption, and blended families of all types. It's important to understand the different types of ownership so you know when a change may be needed.

Joint Ownership

There are three ways to hold assets jointly.

JOINT WITH RIGHTS OF SURVIVORSHIP

The right of survivorship dictates what happens to the co-owned property after one of its owners dies. This title states two or more parties have simultaneous ownership. At the death of one of the joint tenants, ownership of the remaining property passes to the surviving owner and takes precedence over other claims upon the property. The will cannot redirect ownership of property held in this form.

JOINT TENANTS IN COMMON

Tenants in common means there is a divided interest, although none of the owners may claim to own a specific part of the property. At the death of one of the joint owners, the share owned by the deceased must pass through his or her will to determine ownership. The surviving joint owner doesn't automatically own the entirety of assets.

JOINT TENANCY BY THE ENTIRETY

This type of joint ownership is similar to rights of survivorship for married couples. It allows spouses to own property together as a single legal entity. Under a tenancy by the entirety, ownership cannot be separated, which means creditors of an individual spouse may not attach and sell the property. Only creditors of the couple may make claims against the property.

Sole Ownership

The disposition of single name assets is controlled by a will. It could also be controlled through a transfer on death (TOD) designation or payable on death (POD). Adding a TOD designation allows you to pass the securities you own directly to another person or entity without having to go through probate. POD designations do the same thing for bank accounts. Establishing accounts with a TOD or POD designation bypasses the executor or administrator of your estate. The beneficiaries must take steps to re-register the account into their names.

Contractual

This type of account passes to named beneficiaries (in the contract). Commonly held contractual accounts are annuities, life insurance policies, employer-sponsored retirement accounts (401(k)s, 403(b)s, and 457 plans), and individual retirement accounts like IRAs and Roth IRAs. The will only controls disposition of contractual accounts if no beneficiary is specified or if the estate is named as beneficiary.

In Trust

There are many types of trusts that can be established to take ownership of assets. The type of trust you choose will vary depending on what you want to accomplish and can have a significant impact on income and estate taxes. Providing details on the many different types of trusts is well beyond the scope of this book. For simplicity, we refer to a revocable living trust, which would allow one or more persons to be trustees. In this respect, the trust functions similarly to joint ownership with rights of survivorship. The final disposition of the asset will be determined by the terms of the trust.

Community Property

This type of title may only be used by married couples in community property states (Arizona, California, Idaho, Louisiana, Nevada, New Mexico, Texas, Washington, and Wisconsin). Each person owns an undivided interest in the entire property. When one spouse dies the survivor automatically receives the entire interest, avoiding the need for probate. Property titled as community property will not be controlled by a person's will or trust. There is a benefit from a capital gains tax standpoint in that the entire property (not just the half belonging to the deceased spouse) will receive a step up in basis on death.

––––––

The form of ownership in which you take title to property can significantly affect the way the property is taxed, passed to others at death, or divided in the event of divorce. There are benefits and consequences to taking title to property. Your circumstances will merit the value (or cost) that you place on each of these forms of ownership. It is important to take time to consider exactly how you intend to use, and ultimately transfer, the asset before titling it.

Gifting Strategies for Minimizing Estate Taxes

A surefire way to avoid paying tax on your estate is to give your money away as gifts while you're still living. Several gifting strategies exist that can help you accomplish this. In this section, I cover some of the most effective strategies.

Annual Gift Tax Exclusion

One of the simplest estate-planning strategies is to take advantage of the annual gift exclusion, which, in 2016, is $14,000 (this amount is indexed to inflation each year in $1,000 increments). If, for example, a husband and wife gave $14,000 to each of their three children every year, that would be $28,000 per child, times three, for a total of $84,000 given tax free every year. Any grandchildren could also be given the same amount. A couple with a large estate who have several children and grandchildren could make sizable gifts every year to help keep their estate from getting too large.

529 College Savings Plan

Helping your grandchildren save for college by contributing to 529 College Savings Plans for them is an excellent way to give tax-free gifts from your estate. A 529 plan is a tax-advantaged investment account designed to encourage saving for the future higher education expenses of a designated beneficiary. Federal law allows you to contribute to each 529 account with a different beneficiary up to five times the annual gift tax exclusion amount in one year. 529 plans allow the earnings to grow tax-deferred, and distributions for the beneficiary's college costs are exempt from tax. Two of my clients, Bill and Audrey Jennings, took great advantage of this strategy, as demonstrated by the following case study.

CASE STUDY

Bill and Audrey Jennings, retirees

Bill and Audrey Jennings had four adult children and seven grandchildren. Their estate was valued at a little more than $5 million, and they wanted to start an annual gifting program. They decided they wanted to primarily gift to the grandchildren, because they were leaving the estate to their children. All of the grandchildren were minors, and Bill and Audrey were concerned about how the money would be used once the grandchildren turned 21 and gained access to the funds.

They decided to gift their money into 529 College Savings Plans. Their contributions weren't deductible from their federal income tax

RICK'S TIP: Many other states, like Pennsylvania, provide an income-tax deduction for residents who contribute to 529 College Savings Plans.

return, as Pennsylvania residents, though they could take a state income tax deduction for all or part of their contribution.

Because Bill and Audrey could each make gifts as individuals (rather than as a couple), their total contribution to each grandchild could be 10 times the annual gift tax exclusion amount, or $140,000, to each grandchild. A gift tax return would need to be filed to use this provision. If they took advantage of the accelerated gift provision, any further gifts made to the same grandchild during the five-year period may be subject to gift taxes.

Another advantage from Bill and Audrey's perspective was they, as donors, maintained control of the accounts. With few exceptions, the named beneficiary to a 529 plan has no rights to the funds. Most plans even allow donors to reclaim the funds for themselves any time they want.

If you decide to go with a 529 strategy, remember a potential drawback is withdrawals from the account must be spent on eligible college expenses. Money spent for any other purpose will be subject to income tax plus an additional 10% federal tax penalty on the earnings.

Unlimited Gift Tax Exclusion for Tuition

You can also make tax-free estate gifts for your grandchildren's college expenses in another way: through the unlimited gift tax exclusion allowed for tuition you pay directly to a qualifying educational organization. It doesn't matter what your relationship is to the beneficiary to use this exclusion. The exception doesn't apply to expenses like books, dormitory fees, or room and board. You can also use this exclusion to pay healthcare providers directly for medical care for someone else, and payments for medical insurance also qualify for the unlimited gift tax exclusion. Note using these exclusions doesn't have an impact on the $14,000 annual gift tax exclusion limit; you'd still be able to gift up to $14,000 per year to the same person.

RICK'S TIP: If you reclaim the funds you've given to a 529 plan, keep in mind the earnings will be subject to income tax and a 10% penalty tax.

Trusts

A big drawback to using gifting as an estate-planning strategy lies in the fact that to get assets out of your estate, you must give them away and/or give up control. In fact, one of the tests the IRS uses to determine if an asset should be included in your estate is whether or not you've retained any ownership interest. For example, putting money into a custodial account for a minor is a completed gift. However, if you name yourself as the custodian of the account until the minor turns age 21, you've retained control of the account. The value of the custodial account will be included in your estate.

The primary reason we use trusts in estate planning is to give property away but not give up total control. Therefore, caution is advised when pursuing one of the trust strategies I describe.

Review Existing Trust Documents

Many trusts were written back when the estate-tax exemption was less than $1 million. Older trusts were written with less flexibility than the ones written in recent years. Some trusts may be based on

RICK'S TIP: The IRS is constantly looking to shoot down the use of trusts in estate planning. It's imperative you work with a competent estate planner to make sure you follow all the rules to the letter.

outdated tax laws, and others may reflect an era when one spouse had little experience with, or exposure to, financial matters. Those who have trust provisions in their wills should review them to see if they still meet their needs. Trusts drafted today may make it easier to generate income for the surviving spouse by giving the trustee the ability to convert the trust to a private unitrust. This provision allows a trust to invest for total return and distribute a fixed percentage of the value (3–5%, for example) to the income beneficiary. Another common provision allows the trustee to make equitable adjustments between principal and income. The trustee allocates some principal to income and distributes it to the surviving spouse, the income beneficiary. Most states allow both conversions to private unitrusts and equitable adjustments.

CASE STUDY
Mary Ellen Carter, retired widow

I met Mary Ellen to review her finances and offer recommendations on how she could improve her situation. The current low interest rate environment was causing problems for many retirees and this widow's situation was similar. Her main financial goal was to increase her income.

A large portion of her income was coming from a trust established when her husband died more than 10 years prior. This was a typical credit shelter trust paying income to the surviving spouse during her lifetime. All principal was to be distributed to the children after the death of the second spouse. The husband named a local bank as irrevocable trustee. The trust worked well in the beginning when interest rates were higher. When interest rates had fallen to 40-year lows and Mary Ellen's expenses had steadily increased due to inflation, the trust was not producing enough income.

The bank trustee refused to make changes to the investment allocation in favor of producing more income. This is a common problem because the trustee has a conflict between serving the income interests of the survivor and growth interests of the beneficiaries. Most corporate trustees have a maximum allocation to income or growth investments. Once that maximum is reached there is little they are willing to do to alter the portfolio.

Those with existing trust problems are in a difficult situation. Gaining access to the trust principal may depend on the cooperation of the trustee and the other beneficiaries. The children will be agreeing to reduce their future inheritance. Even if all the trust beneficiaries come to an understanding, the trustee may also need to be persuaded. Most corporate trustees are reluctant to do anything other than what is specifically allowed for in the trust. However, with the cooperation of the trustee and beneficiaries a non-judicial settlement may be possible. The trustee and the beneficiaries can agree to modify the trust or to give the trustee a desirable power that's not in the original trust agreement. Such powers can allow the trustee to add the provisions mentioned earlier to address a surviving spouse's income needs. This agreement can be for any purpose, except that it cannot modify a material purpose of the trust.

This solution was not possible in Mary Ellen's case. Some of the beneficiaries were children from another marriage who wouldn't agree with changing the trust. Her income needs would have to be addressed in other ways.

The best time to change a trust is before it becomes irrevocable. Review your trust provisions on a regular basis (every three to five years is recommended) or anytime there is a major change in estate law. Older trusts should be updated to give your heirs the flexibility they may need to avoid coming up short in years to come.

Insurance Trusts

Insurance is commonly misused in estate planning. People often implement an insurance strategy because insurance proceeds bypass probate costs and go directly to the beneficiary, and the death benefit itself is generally not subject to estate taxes. However, the value of the death benefit may be included in the value of the estate, making other assets subject to estate tax. This problem is created when the insured and the policy owner are the same person. The policy owner has ownership rights, and therefore the IRS deems the policy value will be included in the estate.

Another reason an insurance strategy is often implemented in estate planning is to create liquidity in order to pay the estate tax. Liquidity is frequently needed when a significant portion of the estate is a closely held business or a valuable real estate holding, such as a family farm. We also come across the need to provide liquidity when a significant asset is a tax-deferred retirement account. In the story you read about the Richardsons in the Introduction, the heirs were forced to withdraw money from Frank's retirement account to pay the estate taxes, because the only other asset in the estate was the business ownership that couldn't be easily sold. The distribution itself was subject to income taxes, which started a tax spiral that ended up consuming more than 80% of Frank's retirement account.

To avoid these situations, an insurance trust can be created to both generate liquidity and remove the policy from the estate. Consider the following case study about Jay and Evelyn Roberts.

CASE STUDY

Jay and Evelyn Roberts, retirees

The estate of Jay and Evelyn Roberts had passed the $10 million mark. The estate consisted of a farm valued at $5 million, retirement accounts of $2 million, and $5 million in various bank and investment accounts. At the time of the first spouse's death, their estate filed a timely estate tax return in order to make a portability election and report the amount of the unused exemption from the decedent as a carryover to the surviving spouse. This accomplished the goal of preserving each of their lifetime credits.

Jay and Evelyn's total estate of $12 million would have been left with only $1.14 million taxable after the lifetime credit was applied. The heirs' federal estate tax bill would be $456,000. There were sufficient liquid assets in the bank and investment accounts to pay the bill. At this point, they might have considered an aggressive gifting strategy to their children and grandchildren to reduce the taxable portion of the estate. They also could've explored select charities to support, exempting the charitable portion from estate taxes.

Instead, a life insurance agent talked them into buying a $1 million policy on Evelyn's life to provide cash to pay the estate tax. What this agent accomplished was to inflate the estate by $1 million, which raised the federal estate tax bill to $856,000. The policy was owned by Evelyn, and she was also the insured, so their estate was ultimately valued at $13 million—and $2.14 million was taxed at 40%.

In this case, Jay and Evelyn ultimately had plenty of liquid assets, so an insurance policy wasn't necessary for estate liquidity. After all, it didn't make a lot of sense for them to spend $80,000 per year for insurance premiums when they could have simply given the $80,000 outright to their heirs.

If Jay and Evelyn hadn't had plenty of liquid assets, the proper way for them to have used insurance would've been to first establish an irrevocable life insurance trust (ILIT), which would own the policy and also serve as beneficiary. The Roberts would gift the premium payments to the trust. In this way, an ILIT becomes a great technique to use when the estate holds large amounts of illiquid assets. Typically, we'd use a second-to-die policy. The policy would be based on both Jay's and Evelyn's lives, but the death benefit wouldn't be paid until the last one passed away. (The proceeds aren't needed to pay estate taxes until the second spouse dies in this situation.) Second-to-die insurance doesn't cost as much, because it's based on two lives instead of one.

The gifting limits must still be observed when using an insurance trust. The premium payments for Evelyn's policy were $80,000 per year. They have three children who would all be listed as equal beneficiaries under the trust. While both Jay and Evelyn were living, they could gift $28,000 to each child, for a total of $84,000 in tax-free gifts. This amount would cover the premiums required to support the policy.

RICK'S TIP: Remember that the IRS doesn't like trusts for estate planning. In order to keep the policy out of the estate, the beneficiaries have to be given the opportunity to withdraw the money gifted to the policy for premium payments. The withdrawal right is limited for a period of 30 days. Beneficiaries are asked to sign a letter stating they've been given the opportunity to withdraw the gift and have chosen to decline the right. These letters are called "Crummey letters." The term is taken from the case *Crummey v. Commissioner,* which defined the process.

Grantor Retained Annuity Trust

Grantor Retained Annuity Trusts (GRATs) represent yet another type of trust that can be used to protect an estate from taxes. An example of this strategy used by my clients Jerry and Sylvia Anderson follows.

CASE STUDY

Jerry and Sylvia Anderson, retirees

Jerry and Sylvia Anderson had an estate valued at $6 million, which was comprised of their $1 million home and $5 million worth of securities. Each had sizable pension and Social Security incomes that provided all of the money they needed to maintain their lifestyle. When the Andersons both turned 70, they became concerned by the amount of estate tax that would be due upon their deaths. They only had one child, so the most they could gift tax-free was $28,000 per year. The $5 million investment account would earn far more than the amount they could gift.

> **RICK'S TIP:** The interest rate used isn't arbitrary; it's established by the Internal Revenue Code Section 7520 and changes monthly. The IRS recognizes the value of the future income reduces the present value of the gift.

The technique we chose was to use some of their lifetime gifting exclusion of $5.45 million. They could simply gift $2 million to their son, which would reduce their estate and minimize the amount of future growth. We also wanted the technique to allow us to discount the present value of the gift in order to give larger sums of money.

The Andersons' strategy began by establishing an irrevocable trust for their son that paid income back to the couple over a period of time. We determined the trust would make distributions of 5% per year for a period of 10 years.

The Andersons were able to gift $2.4 million to the trust, but it counted only as a gift of $973,000. At the end of the 10 years, the balance remaining in the trust would go directly to their son. If the trust actually earned 8% over the 10 years, the son would receive $3.2 million at the end of the term. The Andersons could also gift back $28,000 per year of the payments using the annual tax-free exclusion, which would amount to another $280,000 passed tax-free to their son. In addition, the annual gifting would also minimize the amount of growth that would accumulate in their own estate from the annuity payments. The Andersons would need to file a gift tax return claiming the present value of the trust and using it against their lifetime exclusions.

Gifting Strategies to Minimize Estate Taxes

- You can achieve substantial estate tax savings by making use of the $14,000 annual gift tax exclusion for gifts to individuals.
- It's important to remember you're legally transferring your wealth to someone else. The tax savings is for your heirs, not you.
- Remember when making gifts of appreciated assets to individuals that they receive the asset at the donor's cost for capital gains tax purposes. Calculate whether the capital gains tax or the estate/inheritance tax will be less before making a gift of this kind.

Be aware there's one big catch to the GRAT strategy: The IRS takes the position the entire value of the trust must be added to the Andersons' estate if they die during the term of the GRAT.

Estate Planning With a Roth IRA

Earlier in this book, we talked a lot about how the Roth IRA is a great tool to use in your retirement savings plan. This extends to estate plans as well, because the Roth IRA can optimize estate plans for taxpayers with significant assets in retirement plans. If you count yourself among this group, a Roth IRA has the potential to provide a great source of wealth for your heirs.

Let's examine the advantages of a Roth IRA in an estate plan by taking a look at the choices of two different men: Dave Kline and Bob Costa.

CASE STUDY

Dave Kline and Bob Costa, estate holders

Dave Kline had a $300,000 IRA he elected to convert to a Roth IRA. He determined that his other retirement assets—including his pension, Social Security, and $500,000 in after-tax savings—would be sufficient to provide all of his income needs throughout his life expectancy. Dave's plan was to allow the Roth to accumulate without taking distributions and spend down his after-tax savings. He anticipated that when the time came to settle his estate, his Roth IRA would represent the most significant asset in his estate and he'd have fewer assets in the after-tax account.

Bob Costa also had a $300,000 IRA he elected to retain to avoid paying a huge tax bill on a Roth conversion. Once Bob turned 70½, his IRA would begin to diminish as he took the annual required minimum distributions. Bob anticipated that when his estate was settled, the IRA would represent a smaller amount because of the minimum distributions. A larger portion of his estate would be in his after-tax accounts. The after-tax assets most likely wouldn't be touched, because the IRA distributions should be sufficient to meet Bob's income needs.

Let's run some projections to quantify the advantages of Dave's conversion and determine how both Bob's and Dave's money will grow and be used throughout their lifetimes. We'll start by comparing the projected outcomes from these two situations.

We'll assume Dave begins converting his IRA at age 65 and completes the conversion over three years. We do this so Dave won't pay more than 25% tax in any year. We'll also assume the tax is paid out of the IRA as the account is converted (not recommended). The value of the Roth after conversion is $225,000. Assuming an 8% growth rate, Dave's Roth will grow to $1,050,000 by the time he passes away at age 85.

Bob leaves his IRA untouched until he must start taking minimum distributions at age 70½. His first year distribution is $16,000, 25% is withheld for taxes, and the difference is reinvested in his after-tax accounts, which grows at 6% after-tax. Each year, Bob takes the minimum IRA distribution, withholds the tax, and reinvests the remaining amount in his after-tax account. When Bob passes away at age 85, his IRA has a remaining balance of $663,750. His total minimum distributions since age 70½ have totaled $344,500 after-tax. The distributions have grown to $508,250. The total of Bob's two accounts is $1,172,000.

At the end of both Dave's and Bob's life expectancies, the two estates contain roughly the same value of assets. In fact, Bob's estate is worth $120,000 more than Dave's, which would seem to indicate that holding the IRA would be the better option. However, simply comparing the total number of dollars available to each estate at the time of the owner's death isn't a complete analysis. To fully appreciate the merits of inheriting a Roth IRA, we need to extend the analysis into the next generation.

Measured in immediate purchasing power, the estate containing the Roth IRA has a big advantage over the estate comprised of the pre-tax IRA and after-tax investments. An after-tax dollar in your pocket will buy the same cup of coffee as the dollar in your pocket from a Roth IRA. But the balance remaining in the IRA still has to be taxed before those dollars can be spent. Applying the same 25% tax level to the $663,750 balance in Bob's IRA nets his heirs only $500,000. Dave's Roth now has roughly a $40,000 advantage over Bob's estate measured in immediate purchasing power.

If both sets of heirs were to liquidate the accounts and spend the money, the story would end here. However, when the heirs maintain the accounts and take only the minimum required distributions through their lifetime, the advantage of the Roth IRA conversion stands out even more.

Bob's 60-year-old child starts to take minimum distributions from the IRA, paying tax at the rate of 25% each year. The child's life expectancy ends at age 85, when the net distributions will have totaled $1.5 million. Combining this with the after-tax account brings the total value of Bob's estate to his heir to a little over $2 million.

Dave's 60-year-old child starts taking their minimum distribution from his Roth IRA. The same life expectancy applies to Dave's heir, so when the child reaches age 85, the distributions will have totaled $3.2 million—more than 50% more than Bob's estate that maintained an IRA!

Throughout this book, I've made the case for the Roth IRA and how it should be an integral part of your retirement plan. The level of control over your income taxes is significantly hampered without having a Roth account to draw on. As this section demonstrates, the power of the Roth doesn't end at life expectancy. The potential value Roth IRAs have in an estate is enormous. Making a significant Roth IRA conversion is usually very beneficial for both you and your heirs. I'd argue in favor of a Roth IRA conversion even if the conversion

RICK'S TIP: The challenge of realizing the maximum wealth potential from an inherited Roth IRA will fall to your heirs. It's essential your beneficiaries understand the value is achieved over time, and the Roth IRA should be preserved in its tax-free environment as long as possible.

doesn't significantly impact your retirement income. When your child or grandchild is named as the beneficiary of a Roth IRA, and he or she elects to take only minimum distributions from the Roth, the value of the Roth is substantially greater than the value of the same amount of after-tax funds.

Beneficiaries: Key to Any Solid Estate Plan

For most people, filling in the names of beneficiaries for retirement assets and life insurance policies is an autopilot task. The primary

---

Estate Planning With a Roth IRA

- The Roth IRA in estate planning can be of even greater value to you than it is in your retirement income planning.
- Analysis of an IRA conversion to a Roth should be measured in immediate purchasing power rather than total dollars. Pre-tax dollars and after-tax dollars don't have the same purchasing power.
- Educate your heirs and beneficiaries about the value of taking distributions from the inherited Roth IRA over time. The total wealth generated for them could be measured in the millions!

---

beneficiary is a spouse; secondary is a child or children. Others simply leave the beneficiary designation blank, and few of us think about updating beneficiaries once they're designated. Yet designating and updating beneficiaries is key to estate planning, because it affects how your assets are dispersed after your death and the quality of life for your heirs.

When I have estate-planning sessions with my clients, I often find the same questions crop up consistently. The following are seven of those very common questions, along with my answers for each:

1. **Why is it important to name beneficiaries?** When you designate a beneficiary for your 401(k), IRA, or life insurance policy, the money in those accounts becomes immediately available to the beneficiary upon your death. If you don't name a beneficiary, those assets will probably go into your estate. A probate court would then dispose of the assets in your estate according to your will. However, the probate process can take months, sometimes years—depriving your heirs of access to your assets until the estate is settled.

2. **Doesn't my will override everything else, including named beneficiaries?** On the contrary, if you have a named beneficiary, that designation overrides your will. This is why it's vitally important to keep beneficiaries updated for all of your assets.

3. **Am I required to name my spouse as my beneficiary?** It depends. Most insurance policies and IRAs don't require you to name your spouse as your primary beneficiary. However, most employer-sponsored plans require your spouse to sign a waiver if you choose not to name him or her as your primary beneficiary. If you live in a community property state, your spouse may have rights to the assets in your IRA regardless of whether or not he or she

is named as primary beneficiary. Check with your estate planning adviser for more information.

4. **Are there any advantages to naming my spouse as the primary beneficiary of my retirement assets?** In general, your spouse has more flexibility than a non-spouse. For example, your spouse can roll over your retirement assets to a qualified plan or IRA in his or her own name, thereby delaying required minimum distributions until age 70½. Non-spouse beneficiaries, on the other hand, must either begin taking distributions soon after your death or deplete the account within about five years after you die.

5. **How many beneficiaries can I name?** Many people think they can name only two beneficiaries because two lines appear on most designation forms. But there's no limit to the number of primary or secondary beneficiaries you can name for any plan. If you run out or room on your beneficiary form, ask if you can attach a sheet of paper with additional designations.

6. **Can I name my minor children as beneficiaries?** Yes, but keep in mind if they're minors when you die, some-one will need to be named to manage the assets until the children reach the age of majority. It's possible to set up a trust in your minor children's names and then desig-nate the trust as beneficiary. However, creating and deal-ing with trusts can be complicated. Your estate-planning adviser can help you make decisions about naming your minor children as beneficiaries.

7. **How often should I review my beneficiaries?** Whenever you experience a major life event—marriage, divorce, the birth or adoption of a child, or the death or disability of a loved one—it's a good idea to review your beneficiary designations.

Because talking about death is difficult, many families over-look some basics for helping loved ones cope more easily during a stressful time. Not knowing the location of your will or safe deposit key, for example, can cause unnecessary worries for family members. In addition to creating an estate plan, take the time now to make the arrangements listed below, in order to help your family after your death.

Funeral or Memorial Service Plans

You can save your family members added grief and potential conflict by discussing your wishes with them and leaving precise written instructions regarding the following decisions:

- Burial or cremation.
- Funeral or memorial service.
- Open or closed casket.
- Wake, viewing, or neither.
- Place of burial.
- Flowers or donations to a charity.
- Music and readings for a service.
- Specific information you'd like included in an obituary.

Updated Records

Keep a current list of all of your assets and property. If your heirs are unaware of an insurance policy or investment you own, it could end up being awarded to the state if the rightful owner can't be identified. In addition, keep a file with your most recent account statements, and make sure the executor of your will knows where to find this file.

Important Documents

Store the important documents below in a safe place, and tell your heirs and your executor where they are and how to access them:

Naming and Assisting Beneficiaries

- If you don't designate beneficiaries for your 401(k), IRA, and life insurance policies, the assets may be tied up in probate court for a long time.
- Review your beneficiary designations after any major life change.
- For qualified plans, you may be required to name your spouse as primary beneficiary unless he or she gives written authorization for you to do otherwise.
- You may name as many beneficiaries as you wish.
- Keep a current list of all of your assets and property.
- Consider storing important information in a safe deposit box, fireproof safe, or file cabinet, and make sure the appropriate parties have access or know where to find the key.
- Discuss funeral or memorial service arrangements with your family and leave written instructions.

- Funeral plans.
- Recent statements and beneficiary information for your retirement and/or pension plans.
- Bank account information.
- Will and any trust documents.
- Deeds and title information for any property you own, including real estate and cars.
- Location and contents of all safes and safe deposit boxes.
- Information regarding any stocks, bonds, or mutual funds you own.
- Living will.
- Durable power of attorney.
- Birth certificate and marriage license.

- Military service records, if applicable.
- Social Security number.
- All auto, home, and life insurance policies.
- Mortgage information.
- Most recent tax return

———

We've reached the end of our exploration of the most tax-efficient ways to structure your retirement savings plan. At several points throughout this book, you probably stopped to dream about what your days will be like when you finally retire. I hope you envisioned times when you felt relaxed, enjoyed family and friends, and engaged in activities you love. After working hard for many years, retirement should be one of the best stages of your life and filled with all of these things and more.

Your retirement *should not* involve stress and anxiety about whether you've accumulated enough savings to support yourself in your golden years—or whether the IRS is going to deplete your savings through excessive taxation. The knowledge you've gained throughout the book will help you avoid this stress, because the tax-efficient plan you are going to implement based on your newfound knowledge will both help your retirement assets grow now, and steer the IRS away from taxing those assets later.

Above all, remember one thing: Your New Three-Legged Stool should be balanced among the three primary types of retirement savings plans—pre-tax, after-tax, and tax-free. Not only is it important to strike a balance when establishing and contributing to these accounts, but you must also remain aware of the tax implications involved in withdrawing from the accounts when you retire. If all of this seems daunting, don't worry; there are good financial advisers out there who can help you connect the dots. Just use the tips I gave you to find one.

Here's wishing you and your family a wonderful retirement.

APPENDIX
HOW TO WRITE A PERSONAL
FINANCIAL PLAN

At several points throughout *Don't Retire Broke*, I stress the importance of working with a knowledgeable financial adviser to build and execute your retirement plan. This doesn't mean, however, you can simply sit back and expect your adviser to act entirely on his or her own. Don't forget: You are still the most important person in the process; after all, it's your future!

One of the best ways to achieve success with your financial adviser is to write a personal financial plan. From your professional life, you may be familiar with writing a business plan; the financial plan I'm talking about is like a business plan, except it's for investing. This plan should have two parts. First, it should clearly state the terms of communication you expect to have with your adviser—how and when your adviser will keep you informed about the status of your investments. Second, it should outline your expectations for your investments themselves, defining your financial goals as well as the type of portfolio you'll build to achieve those goals.

Although many investors get only generic recommendations from their advisers, writing a personal financial plan like the kind I've described is your chance to be specific. You'll never regret putting the way you want your account managed in writing. This way, if anything goes wrong, you and your adviser can always refer to your plan to get back on track.

Part One: Establish Clear Adviser-Client Communication

Your financial adviser may be doing a fantastic job of managing your retirement assets, but if the two of you aren't on the same communications page, you could ultimately end up dissatisfied. It's not enough to achieve good returns on your investments; your adviser must also do a good job of keeping you posted on the status of these returns (or lack thereof). Remember: Though you should be able to expect a lot of things from a financial adviser, mind-reading isn't one of them. Sufficient communication means different things to different people, and it's up to you to define your version of good communication to your adviser so she or he has a clear understanding of your expectations.

3 Steps to Establishing Clear Client-Adviser Communication

Follow these three steps to make clear client-adviser communication an official part of your personal financial plan. Don't just have a casual conversation about them with your adviser; put the terms you agree to down on the same paper that contains your expectations for your investments themselves (which we'll talk about in part two below). This way, both you and your adviser will take your communications commitments seriously.

1. **Establish a maximum time frame within which your adviser will return your phone calls.** As with any business, your adviser will likely have many clients but should always do his or her best to make you feel

you're the only one! This means returning your phone calls promptly, which is an immediate indication of responsiveness to your needs. In your plan, be specific about how long it will take for your adviser to get back to you; for example, instead of writing "My calls will be returned promptly," specify "My calls will be returned within two business days"—and hold your adviser to it! Never accept adviser excuses like "I couldn't get back to you because I've been with other clients." Your business is too important for that.

2. **Set a schedule by which you will receive written updates on your portfolio.** Traditionally, financial services firms send their clients written updates on a quarterly basis. Expect no less than this from your adviser, and don't hesitate to ask for more frequent updates if this makes you feel more comfortable. With the convenience of the Internet and email, providing you with frequent updates is easier now than ever.

3. **Come to an agreement about how often you'll meet.** Although you should feel free to call your adviser with your questions as they arise, you can also expect him or her to commit to regularly scheduled status meetings. These meetings ensure your adviser will set aside dedicated time to focus on you and your portfolio, and you should expect to hear a comprehensive, specific update on your portfolio's status each time you get together. Make sure you build in enough time to ask any additional questions you might have after you hear the adviser's report, as well as to do any necessary portfolio adjustments.

Part Two: Create a Detailed Investment Plan

Once you and your adviser have completed the communications portion of your personal financial plan, which will be based on your

RICK'S TIP: Regular portfolio reviews are a critical endeavor for any investor since, as we painfully experienced in the fall of 2008, circumstances in both the financial markets and/or your personal life can cause your goals to change over time.

mutual understanding of how and when you'll communicate, you can move on to writing your investment plan.

This five-step exercise will help you as well as your adviser. Putting your investment thoughts in writing will encourage you to sort through any internal confusion or indecision you may have had about what exactly you want to have achieved upon retirement. It will also help your adviser to comprehend your current and long-term financial concerns and needs. Finally, it will assist both of you by setting forth guidelines for reviewing your goals and risk tolerance on a regular basis.

5 Steps to Creating a Detailed Investment Plan

1. **Define your current and future financial goals.** Any successful financial plan incorporates both long-term goals, like owning a second vacation home and putting all of your kids through college, and short-term goals, such as the amount of money you need to pay your monthly bills. Listing these goals at the beginning of your investment plan will help you structure the plan to meet your needs today and help to ensure you'll reach your goals tomorrow.

2. **Identify a time frame for achieving your goals.** It's fine to determine the lifestyle you want to have someday upon retirement, but if you don't specifically define what you mean by "someday," you're in danger of creating an

investment portfolio that won't meet your long-term goals. As we discussed in Leg Two (Chapter 2), you must design your portfolio to include the right mix of assets that will minimize risk while maximizing returns. This mix is inextricably tied to your retirement time horizon and will vary according to whether you want to retire in five, 10, 15 years—or longer.

3. **Decide on an acceptable rate of return.** Some investors do their due diligence by establishing their investment goals and time horizon, yet they still end up shocked when they receive their first portfolio statement. That's because these investors likely didn't think about how their goals and time frame would translate into regular rates of return—which can be disarming for those who plan to retire later and therefore assume more short-term risk to achieve larger long-term gains. Be sure your adviser spells out the types of return rates you can expect to experience based on your goals and time horizon; if you find you're uncomfortable with these rates, your adviser can help you to tweak your plan so it strikes a good balance between your goals and rate-of-return comfort level.

4. **Outline a specific strategy for asset allocation.** From reading this book, you already know how important it is to structure your investment portfolio around the idea of asset allocation. The mix of asset classes in your portfolio contributes to the rate of return discussed in step 3 above, so it's critical for your adviser to get specific about the types and quantities of assets she or he plans to include in that portfolio. Be sure your plan includes precise details about the combination of the three main asset classes (cash/money markets, bonds, and stocks) you can expect to see in your regular statements. This will prevent ambiguity and provide you and your adviser with a reference point should questions arise later.

5. **Determine methods for monitoring your portfolio.** At this point, you've finished building a solid foundation for your investment plan. But as I mentioned under Part One, changing circumstances can throw a wrench into even the most well-crafted plan. It's imperative, then, that your personal investment plan include rules for regular monitoring of your portfolio's performance by your adviser. This entails defining the benchmarks your adviser will measure your portfolio against, as well as establishing how often your adviser will review your investments. Though the two of you already established a schedule for how often you'll meet, a good adviser will want to review your plan more frequently than right before your meetings, and proactively contact you should he or she discover issues that must be discussed.

Writing a Personal Financial Plan

- Writing a personal financial plan helps you define the financial position you hope to be in upon retirement and provides guidance for the adviser you'll work with to get there.
- You should write your personal financial plan in two parts. Part One revolves around the terms of communication you can expect from your adviser; Part Two includes specifics about how your adviser will allocate your assets and monitor your portfolio's success.
- Make your plan as specific as possible, incorporating precise details wherever you can. The more specificity you include, the less room for confusion—and the better chance for good investment returns.

GLOSSARY

ACA The Patient Protection and Affordable Care Act, commonly called the Affordable Care Act or "ObamaCare."

ADV part II A form that is like a prospectus on an advisory firm, explaining potential conflicts of interest.

AIME Average indexed monthly earnings.

Amortization The process of decreasing or accounting for an amount over a period of time.

AMT (Alternative Minimum Tax) The alternative minimum tax operates in effect as a parallel tax system, with its own definition of taxable income, exemptions, and tax rates. Taxpayers compute tax owed under the "regular" and AMT systems and are liable for whichever is higher. The AMT system has in general a broader definition of taxable income, a larger exemption, and lower tax rates than the regular system.

Annuitization The process of taking an asset and, by way of an installment sale or annuity sale, effectively converting the asset into a stream of payments.

Annuity factor Another phrase for the life-expectancy factor.

ATRA12 American Taxpayer Relief Act of 2012.

BB corporate bond A type of high-yield bond.

CD Certificate of deposit.

Crummey letters A term taken from the case *Crummey v. Commissioner,* which defined the process of having beneficiaries of estate gifts sign a letter stating they've been given the opportunity to withdraw the gift within the 30-day withdrawal-rights period and have chosen to decline the right.

CRUT Charitable remainder unitrust.

DALBAR A firm that develops standards for—and provides research, ratings, and rankings of intangible factors to—the financial services industry.

Efficient frontier The combinations of investments exhibiting the optimal risk/reward trade-off.

ERISA Employee retirement income security act.

FICA Payroll taxes.

FUTA Federal unemployment tax.

GRAT Grantor retained annuity trust.

HSA Health Savings Account.

ILIT Irrevocable life insurance trust.

Junk bond A type of high-yield bond.

MAGI Modified adjusted gross income.

NAV Net asset value.

NUA (Net Unrealized Appreciation) The difference in value between the average cost basis of shares and the current market value of the shares held in a tax-deferred account.

OASDI Old age survivor and disability insurance.

PIA Primary insurance amount.

QCD Qualified IRA Charitable Distribution.

RBD Required beginning date.

R/D Factor The retirement distribution factor, a scale from 0 (the point at which all of your income is taxable) to 100 (where all of your retirement income is tax-free), against which you can measure how well you've done with reducing your taxable retirement income by building a balanced New Three-Legged Stool.

SPD Summary Plan Description.

SSI Social Security Income.

NOTES

Introduction

1. "Summary of Latest Federal Income Tax Data," Tax Foundation, December 18, 2013.
2. Investment Company Institute, December 17, 2014.
3. AARP.
4. "2013 Annual Report to Congress," National Taxpayer Advocate.

Chapter 1

1. *Bobrow v. Commissioner* (T.C. Memo. 2014-21).

Chapter 2

1. Robert M. Dammon, Chester S. Spatt, and Harold H. Zhang, "Optimal Asset Location and Allocation With Taxable and Tax-Deferred Investing," *The Journal of Finance* Vol. LIX, No. 3 (June 2004): 999–1038.
2. Gary P. Brinson, L. Randolph Hood, and Gilbert L. Beebower, "Determinants of Portfolio Performance," *Financial Analysts Journal* Vol. 42, No. 4 (July–August 1986): 39–44.
3. *Qualitative Analysis of Investor Behavior (QAIB) Report 2014*, DALBAR, Inc. Research & Communications Division.
4. *2013 Quantitative Analysis of Investor Behavior*, DALBAR, Inc. Research & Communications Division, page 14.
5. Richard Michaud, "The Markowitz Optimization Enigma: Is 'Optimized' Optimal?" *Financial Analysts Journal* Vol. 45, No. 1 (January–February 1989): 31–42.

6. Nassim Nicholas Taleb, *The Black Swan: The Impact of the Highly Improbable* (New York: Random House, 2007).
7. Raymond F. DeVoe, Jr., *DeVoe Report* (July 1995).
8. *ICI Research Perspective* Volume 19, No 3 (April 2013).
9. Bill Barker, "Turnover and Cash Reserves," The Motley Fool, *www.fool.com/School/MutualFunds/Costs/Turnover.htm*.
10. Brinson, Hood, and Beebower, "Determinants of Portfolio Performance."

Chapter 4

1. "Determining Withdrawal Rates Using Historical Data," *Journal of Financial Planning* (October 1994).
2. "Conserving Client Portfolios During Retirement, Part III," *Journal of Financial Planning* (December 1997).
3. Philip L. Cooley, Carl M. Hubbard, and Daniel T. Walz, "Retirement Savings: Choosing a Withdrawal Rate That Is Sustainable," *AAII Journal* (February 1998).
4. William Bengen, "How Much Is Enough?" *Financial Advisor Magazine* (May 2012).
5. Matrix Book 2012, Dimensional Funds.
6. Sandy Baker, *Your Complete Guide to Early Retirement: A Step-by-Step Plan for Making it Happen* (Atlantic Publishing Company, 2007).

Chapter 5

1. *The 2016 Annual Report of the Board of Trustees of the Federal Old-Age and Survivors Insurance and Federal Disability Insurance Trust Funds.*
2. "Historical Background and Development of Social Security," U.S. Social Security Administration Website, *www.socialsecurity.gov/history/briefhistory3.html* (March 2003).
3. Alicia H. Munnel, PhD, Alex Golub-Sass, and Nadia S. Karamcheva, PhD, "Understanding Unusual Social Security Claiming Strategies," *Journal of Financial Planning* (August 2013).
4. *The 2016 Annual Report.*
5. "2015 OASDI Trustees Report," *www.ssa.gov/oact/tr/2015/II_E_conclu.html#86802.*
6. *Risky Business: Living Longer Without Income for Life* (American Academy of Actuaries, June 2013).
7. Andrew Biggs, "The Distributional Consequences of a "No-Action" Scenario, Social Security Administration," Policy Brief No. 2004-01, *www.ssa.gov/policy/docs/policybriefs/pb2004-01.html#mn6* (2004).

8. Secretary of the Treasury John W. Snow, Prepared Remarks: The Wilmington Club, *www.treasury.gov/press/releases/js2333.htm* (March 24, 2005).

9. *Means Testing for Social Security,* issue brief (American Academy of Actuaries, December 2012).

10. "Option: Begin Means-Testing Social Security Benefits," AARP Public Policy Institute.

Chapter 6

1. "How to Plan for Rising Health Care Costs," Fidelity Viewpoints, *www.fidelity.com/viewpoints/personal-finance/plan-for-rising-health -care-costs.*

2. "Trends in Health Care Cost Growth and the Role of the Affordable Care Act," *www.whitehouse.gov/sites/default/files/docs/healthcostreport _final_noembargo_v2.pdf* (November 2013).

Chapter 7

1. "2011 EZLaw Wills & Estate Planning Survey, LexisNexis®, July 19, 2011.

INDEX

ABOUT THE AUTHOR

Rick Rodgers, CFP® is an author, keynote speaker, wealth manager, and president of Rodgers & Associates, "The Retirement Specialists," in Lancaster, Pennsylvania. Rick's articles on retirement planning have appeared in *Wealth Manager Magazine*, *CPA Magazine*, and *Physician's Money Digest*. Rick has appeared numerous times on WGAL TV and WPMT Fox 43 in York to discuss financial issues in the news. He was called upon by WITF radio for a special appearance on *Smart Talk* in October 2008 to discuss the financial crisis as it was unfolding. He has been quoted in the *New York Times*, *Money Magazine*, *Investment News*, *Smart Money*, *Central Pennsylvania Business Journal*, *Harrisburg Patriot News*, and Lancaster newspapers. In 2015, the Lancaster Chamber of Commerce & Industry named Rick the Small Business Person of the Year at their 143rd Annual Dinner.

Rick is a 30-plus-year industry veteran, beginning his career with Shearson American Express in 1984. He founded Rodgers & Associates, along with his wife, Jessica, in 1996 to help families create and conserve their wealth in preparation for worry-free and dignified retirements. With the commitment to help his clients plan for the future while living in the present, Rick offers an individually focused approach to helping clients reach their retirement goals.

Rick is a 1987 graduate of Leadership Lancaster and is a current member of the prestigious Financial Planning Association. Rodgers & Associates is a corporate member of NAPFA (the National Association of Personal Financial Advisors). A committed Christian, Rick served as a field representative for the North East to Larry Burkett's organization Christian Financial Concepts from 1990 to 1995. Rick and his wife, Jessica, are active supporters of their community. The use of their company's office at The Manor (2025 Lititz Pike, Lancaster) is offered to non-profits who serve the community at no cost to use for luncheons, board meetings, and board retreats. They have co-sponsored Lancaster's Extraordinary Give (*ExtraGive.org*) with the Lancaster County Community Foundation since 2013. They have also been partners with Millersville University since 2011 in support the Ware Center & Winter Center annual programming of visual and performing arts.

Rick can be reached at:

rick@rodgers-associates.com

(717) 560-3800